The Beginner's Guide to Chinese Calligraphy

An Introduction to Semi-Cursive Script (*Xingshu*)

By Zhou Bin
Yi Yuan
Zhou Weiwei

Better Link Press

This book is edited and designed by the Editorial Committee of *Cultural China* series

Text: Zhou Bin, Yi Yuan, Zhou Weiwei
Works: Zhou Bin
Translation: Zhao Gang
Interier and Cover Design: Yuan Yinchang, Li Jing, Hu Bin (Yuan Yinchang Design Studio)

Copy Editor: Susan Luu Xiang
Assistant Editor: Wu Yuezhou
Editor: Yang Xiaohe
Editorial Director: Zhang Yicong

Senior Consultants: Sun Yong, Wu Ying, Yang Xinci
Managing Director and Publisher: Wang Youbu

ISBN: 978-1-60220-139-2

Address any comments about *The Beginner's Guide to Chinese Calligraphy: An Introduction to Semi-Cursive Script* (Xingshu) to:

Better Link Press
99 Park Ave
New York, NY 10016
USA

or

Shanghai Press and Publishing Development Company
F 7 Donghu Road, Shanghai, China (200031)
Email: comments_betterlinkpress@hotmail.com

Printed in China by Shanghai Donnelley Printing Co., Ltd.

3 5 7 9 10 8 6 4 2

Contents

化為生育萬物安之而不知其恩
天下和平災害不生禍
是日也天朗氣清惠風和暢仰
觀宇宙之大俯察品類之盛
日聽有經之師上金六兩白素
六雙青絲六兩五色繒各廿二

Foreword

The beauty of the Chinese written word has many dimensions. There is the fine balance of black and white in the graphic representation and then there are the many layers of historical, literary, and cultural meanings of the word itself. How can a student new to Chinese ever hope to fully appreciate such beauty? The authors draw the viewer into the world of Chinese characters, opening little doors on every dimension, allowing the students to explore and discover the beauty on their own.

Prof. Zhou taught students from many different backgrounds in the course "Brush with Peace" at Lehigh University. Some learned to love Chinese through the meditative practice of simply replicating aesthetically balanced graphs using the same medium—brushes, ink, and paper—that Chinese artists and scholars have used for millennia. This intimate experience with China's rich literary history filled them with awe. Students who had more knowledge of the Chinese language, the words behind the graphs, had the opportunity to move deeper into this experience. They not only felt the inner peace of this ancient brush art but also began the educational journey of learning the multi-layered meanings and contexts over time. After these classes were finished, many students came to me begging for more. This book serves as a first step to that "more." Learning Chinese brush arts is a gateway to beauty and peace. It is a gift to the world from China.

Prof. C. A. Cook
Lehigh University

長嘯草木震動山鳴谷
起水涌余亦悄然而悲肅
恐凜乎其不可留也返
放乎中流聽其所止而休
夜將半四顧寂寥適有
橫江東來翅如車輪玄

Preface

In 2011, before I started my journey to New York University for research in cross-cultural psychology in Chinese calligraphy education, I received a lot of letters from Chinese Language teachers in the United States asking me to give them some guidance on calligraphy teaching. A teacher from Perkiomen School in Pennsylvania told me by email that all his students wanted to learn Chinese calligraphy and he hoped that they could get the chance to learn from me during my one-year stay in New York. He also said that he would like to bring his students to New York every week for this purpose. I was deeply moved.

During my time in New York, the total number of my calligraphy students exceeded three hundred. Each semester, over one hundred university students took calligraphy as an elective course. However, as calligraphy set a high requirement for the classroom, only half of the students could attend the class. Calligraphy became a top priority of American students interested in learning Chinese culture.

As a distinctive art of words, calligraphy can record the Chinese language, bring into play the aesthetic function of art and culture, and mould a person's temperament. This last function has been gaining increasing recognition worldwide.

People who love Chinese culture for the unique practical value, artistic quality, and cultural concepts it conveys have valued Chinese calligraphy. However, as traditional Chinese culture and Western culture belong to two different cultural systems, and the ways to think and understand things between the East and West are different, people who are interested in but are not familiar with Chinese culture may encounter huge difficulties or intimidating barriers in the initial learning process due to their lack of knowledge in Chinese history, religion, philosophy, etc. During my research at New York University from 2011 to 2012, I conducted a relatively thorough study on American learners of Chinese calligraphy at different levels and found that textbooks of Chinese calligraphy with an emphasis on bridging cultural differences were very small in number. This has finally given rise to this book.

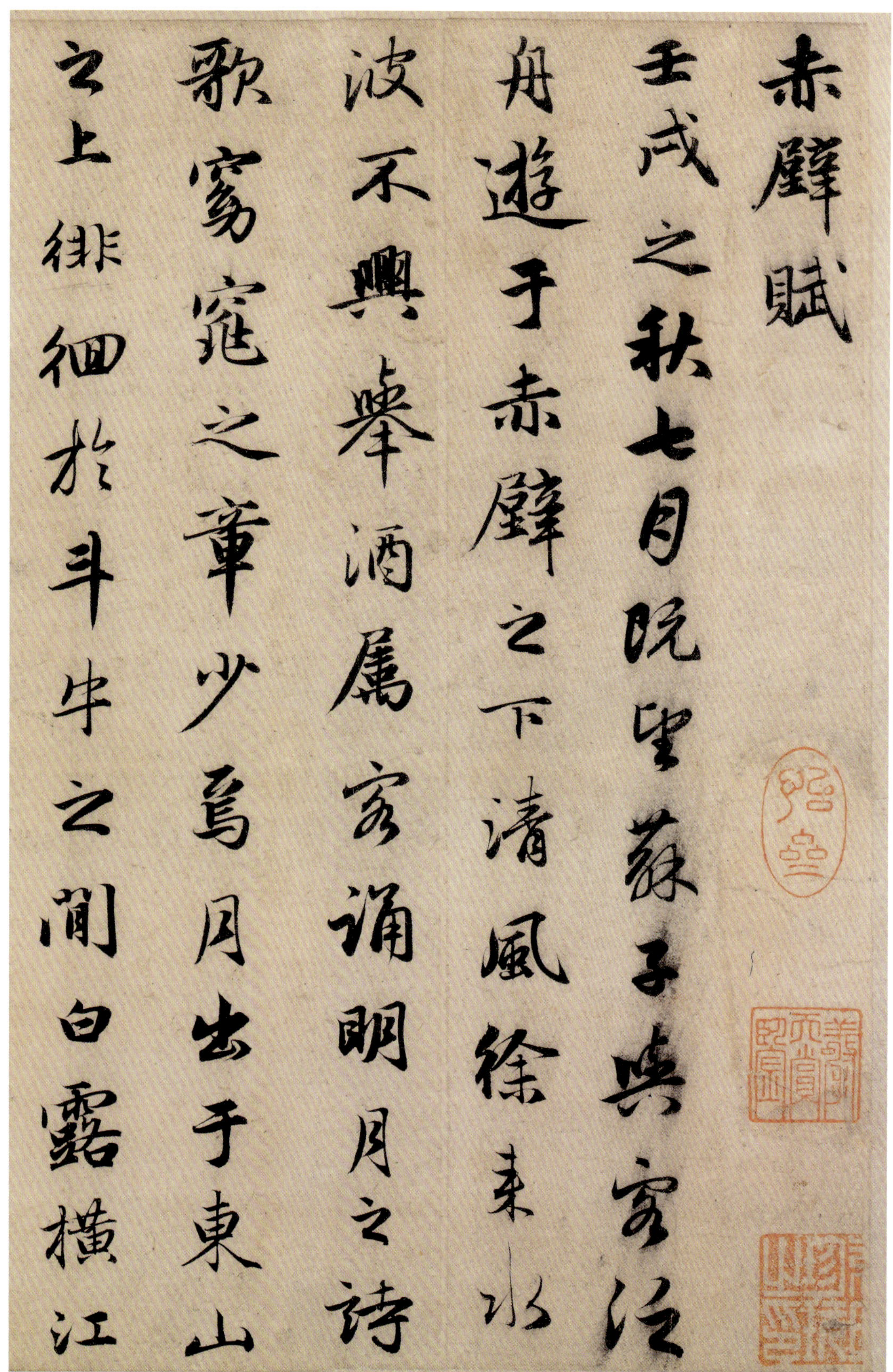
赤壁賦
壬戌之秋七月既望蘇子與客泛
舟遊于赤壁之下清風徐來水
波不興舉酒屬客誦明月之詩
歌窈窕之章少焉月出于東山
之上徘徊於斗牛之間白露橫江

Figure 1
The *First and Second Odes to Red Cliffs* is one of the famous semi-cursive works writtern by Zhao Mengfu, the most renowned calligrapher of Yuan Dynasty.

This book illustrates the history and techniques of Chinese calligraphy using concepts understandable to Western readers. It has the specific following features.

1. Easy to understand. Using clear language, this book reveals the cultural deposits of Chinese calligraphy based on a discussion of some classical Chinese calligraphic works. Take for example the *First and Second Odes to Red Cliffs* (前后赤壁赋, *Qian Hou Chi Bi Fu*) by Su Shi (1037 – 1101), one of the most famous literati in the Song Dynasty (Figure 1). Instead of directly analyzing the style of this work and the reasons behind it, the book starts with the story of the Battle of the Red Cliffs fought in 208 in an effort to provide Western readers with the relevant background knowledge.

2. Steady in progress. Taking into full consideration the cognitive rules for people of different cultural backgrounds to learn foreign cultures, this book proceeds steadily from simple to complicated and from easy to difficult. For example, in the section about the writing techniques of semi-cursive script, it starts with the basic strokes of Chinese characters, moves on to combined strokes and the art of composition, and concludes with calligraphy creation. In addition, the chapters and relevant knowledge in the book are arranged logically to effectively maximize teaching and learning.

3. Vivid in presentation. Pictures and calligraphic works are selected to match the text descriptions in an effort to vividly present some difficult points in Chinese calligraphic culture, and reduce readers' difficulty in learning Chinese calligraphy.

I choose semi-cursive script for this book mainly because this script is practical for daily use and enjoys high artistic quality. Finding that they can quickly apply the writing techniques they have acquired from this book to their writing practice, learners will have a greater sense of achievement.

Calligraphic works of Zhao Mengfu (1254 – 1322) are the main examples for analysis in this book, because the "Zhao-style calligraphy" is a model of semi-cursive script and represents the fusion of Confucianism and Taoism. As a typical type with features of the most basic regular script, Zhao-style semi-cursive script is simple and easy to learn.

The teaching concept embodied in this book has been widely recognized and its content has been used in quite a number of prestigious U.S. universities, such as Lehigh University, New York University, and Columbia University, and international organizations, such as the United Nations and China Institute.

I am indebted to Professor Frank Tang at New York University and Professor C. A. Cook at Lehigh University for their invaluable advice and suggestions during the writing of this book. I would also like to thank my postgraduate students Yang Shuang and Cai Yangyang for the hard work they have put into this book.

Zhou Bin

江流有聲斷岸千尺山高
水落石出曾日月之幾何
川不可復識矣余乃攝衣
履巉巖披蒙茸踞虎
虯龍攀棲鶻之危巢俯
之幽宮蓋二客不能從焉

Chapter One

Chinese Calligraphy and Semi-Cursive Script

Chinese calligraphy is the art of writing with Chinese characters as a means to express feelings and sentiments. There is a general standardization of the various styles of calligraphy in this tradition that were developed in the past thousands years.

1. A Brief History of Chinese Calligraphy

In its history of over 3,000 years, Chinese calligraphy has evolved from inscriptions on oracle bones, drum-shaped stone blocks, and ancient bronze objects to large seal script (*dazhuan*), small seal script (*xiao-zhuan*), clerical script (*lishu*), cursive script (*caoshu*), regular script (*kaishu*), and semi-cursive script (*xing-shu*). Calligraphers across dynasties have kept on improving their writing techniques and diversifying their aesthetic pursuits, rendering Chinese calligraphy with richer cultural connotations and an endlessly dynamic life.

Using such special writing tools as the writing brush, ink, paper, and ink-slab, and allowing their feelings to control the direction of their brush, the force of lift and press, and the dryness and moistness of ink, calligraphers have displayed the ever-changing patterns of lines. "Black lines on white paper" is a perfect interpretation of the concept of symbiosis between yin and yang in Chinese philosophy, simple but profound.

A series of aesthetic factors are emphasized in Chinese calligraphy, i.e. the way the writing brush is held and wielded, the strokes and spatial structure of the character, and the art of character composition. Meanwhile, like other forms of art, calligraphy demonstrates a high level of human thinking. A calligraphic work is a physical portrayal of the calligrapher's feelings and thoughts, and his calligraphic style often mirrors his self-cultivation and moral conduct. This is exactly what people mean when they say, "Just as the handwriting reveals the writer, so a person is known through his calligraphy."

2. Origin and Evolution of Semi-Cursive Script

In tracing the history of Chinese characters, one can detect a clear line of evolution from inscriptions on oracle bones, large seal script, and small seal script to clerical script. However, the formation and development of clerical script, cursive script, semi-cursive script, and regular script are more complicated, as they, while developing side by side, tend to influence each other.

The Eastern Han Dynasty: Start of Semi-Cursive Script

According to *Evaluation of Calligraphy* (书断, *Shu Duan*), a book on the evaluation of calligraphers and calligraphic works, authored by Zhang Huaiguan (dates unknown, active in 713 – 714), a famous calligraphy theoretician in the Tang Dynasty, semi-cursive script is created by Liu Desheng. Liu

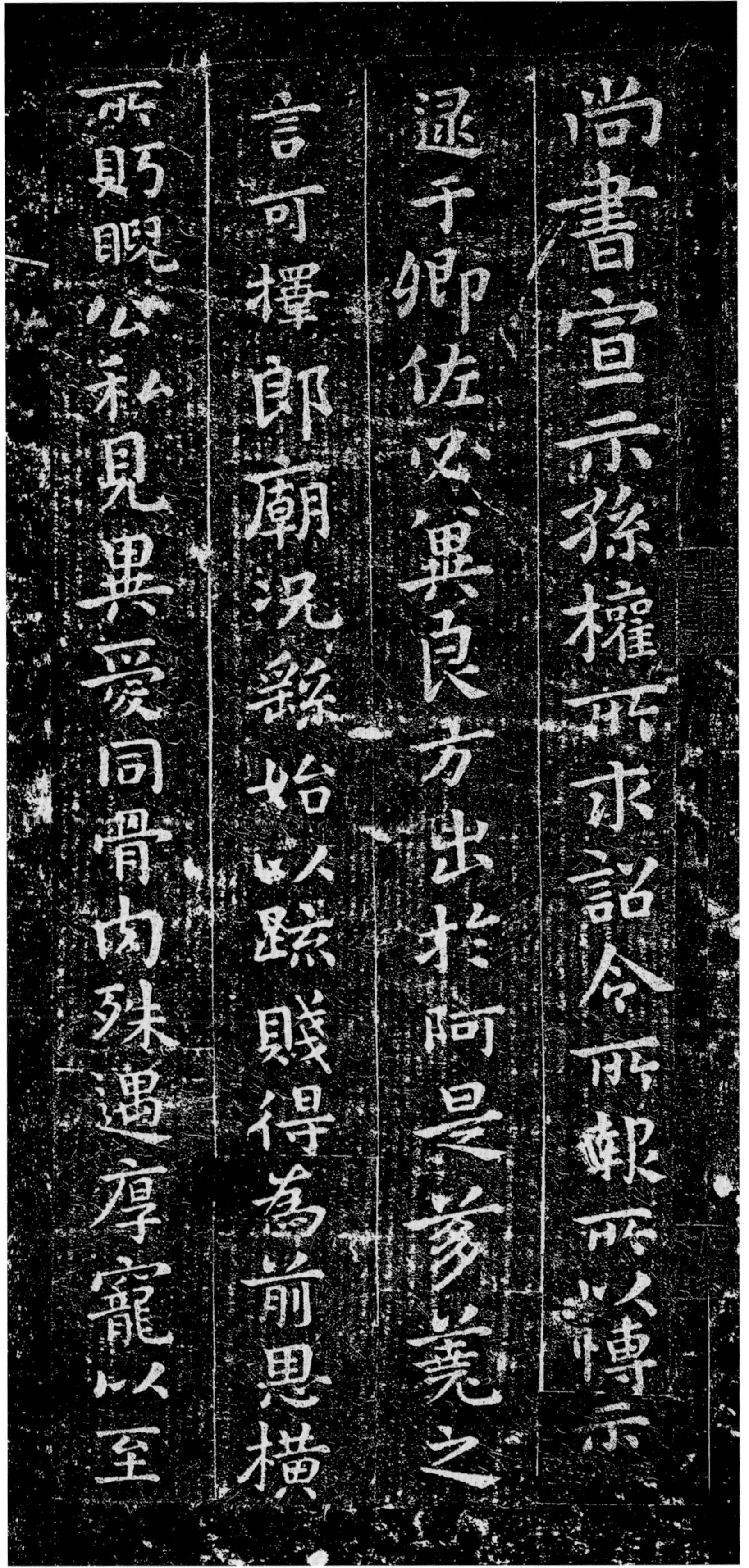

Desheng (c. 147 – 189), a native of Yingchuan (in today's Xuchang, Henan province), was indeed a well-versed calligrapher in the late Eastern Han Dynasty (25 – 220). However, none of his calligraphic works, in whatever form, have been passed down and no other physical evidence has shown that it was he who created semi-cursive script.

Nevertheless, Zhong Yao (151 – 230), one of the students of Liu Desheng, is a prestigious calligrapher. Zhong Yao, also a native of Yingchuan, occupies a prominent position in the calligraphic history and has gained remarkable achievements in regular and semi-cursive scripts (Figure 2).

Current research forcibly show that semi-cursive script was not

Figure 2
***Memorial to the Emperor for the Acceptance of Other's Surrender* (宣示表, *Xuan Shi Biao*)**
Zhong Yao (151 – 230, Wei, Three Kingdoms)
Regular script

Known as the earliest example of regular script, *Memorial to the Emperor for the Acceptance of Other's Surrender* was written with vigorous simplicity and natural grace. The waves of the right-falling strokes still have the features of clerical script, looking dignified yet quaint. The characters are simple in structure, steady, and graceful.

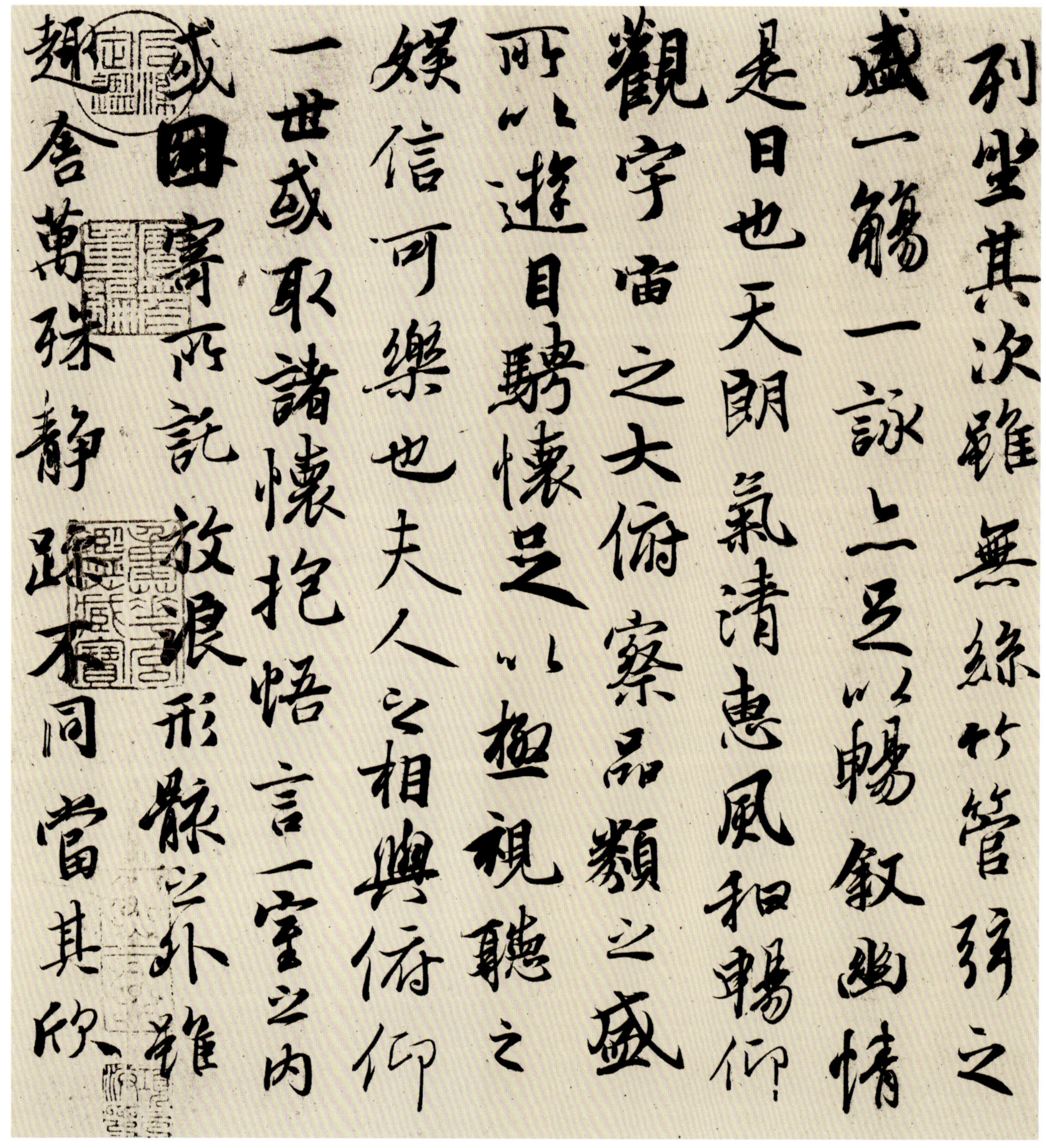

Figure 3
Preface to the Orchid Pavilion Collection (兰亭序, *Lan Ting Xu*)
Wang Xizhi (303 – 361, or 321 – 379, Eastern Jin Dynasty)
Semi-cursive script
24.5 cm × 69.9 cm
Palace Museum, Beijing

On March 3, the 9th year of Yonghe (353), Wang Xizhi, along with his friend Xie An (320 – 385) and 40 others, was present at a gathering at the Orchid Pavilion, enjoying wine and composing poems. Wang was suggested to make an edited collection of these poems and compose a preface to record this event and his own feelings. Known as *Preface to the Orchid Pavilion Collection*, this calligraphy work is acclaimed to be "the best semi-cursive script in the world." It reflects the Chinese philosophical concept of "being naturally formed" and achieves a high degree of harmony between content and form through the calligrapher's diverse and refined use of the writing brush. The authentic piece is already lost, and the current ones are all imitations by calligraphers of later generations.

invented by one person alone. It emerged in the late Eastern Han Dynasty, gradually gained popularity with the concerted efforts of such calligraphers as Liu Desheng and Zhong Yao, and finally became today's dynamic and popular script of Chinese calligraphy.

Sun Guoting (646 – 691), the most famous calligraphy reviewer in the Tang Dynasty, once observed accurately in his representative work *Treatise on Calligraphy* (书谱, *Shu Pu*), "Semi-cursive script is highly recommended for calligraphers looking to adapt to current fashions and changes." Semi-cursive script, as a form of calligraphy, is capable of adjusting itself to the changes of the social and humanistic environment and making breakthroughs in this process. It has undergone three changes in style in the history of its development.

The Wei and Jin Dynasties: Fixing the Direction of Development

Indisputably, semi-cursive script took its first leap in development in the Wei and Jin dynasties (220 – 420), an extremely important period in the history of Chinese calligraphy when all types of calligraphy prospered.

Wang Xizhi (303 – 361 or 321 – 379) and Wang Xianzhi (344 – 386), father and son, were the most outstanding calligraphers of this period. As a family of calligraphers, the Wangs enjoyed a fine atmosphere of learning at home. Wang Xizhi learned calligraphy as a child, gradually comprehended its essence after touring many famous mountains and great rivers and seeing with his own eyes the stone inscriptions of the authentic handwritings of prestigious calligraphers, and finally reached a level of acheivement that "surpassed all other calligraphers before and since." Wang Xizhi is said to have produced over a thousand calligraphic works; however, none of them have survived the changes of time and all his works we see today are imitations by calligraphers of later generations. His highest calligraphic achievement is in semi-cursive script, the best of which is *Preface to the Orchid Pavilion Collection*, which is known as "the world's best semi-cursive script" (Figure 3).

Wang Xianzhi was the seventh son of Wang Xizhi. Influenced by his family, he started to learn calligraphy at a very young age. His exceptional talent in calligraphy and unrelenting diligence enabled him to create a unique style of his own in running-cursive script (*xingcaoshu*), a style between semi-cursive and cursive scripts. Enjoying equal prestige, father and son reached a summit in calligraphy insurmountable by other calligraphers either in the Wei and Jin periods or in Chinese calligraphic history.

Though both were masters of calligraphy, Wang Xizhi and Wang Xianzhi were sharply different in calligraphic style. The father wrote easily and smoothly, emphasizing variety and the beauty of harmony. The son, on the contrary, was bold in character composition, wrote casually but with distinct individuality, and pursued the grace of motion (Figure 4). Their different styles gave rise to the "contained" and "unrestrained" writing techniques, which have exerted a far-reaching influence on the development of semi-cursive script.

The calligraphic skill Wang Xizhi and his son

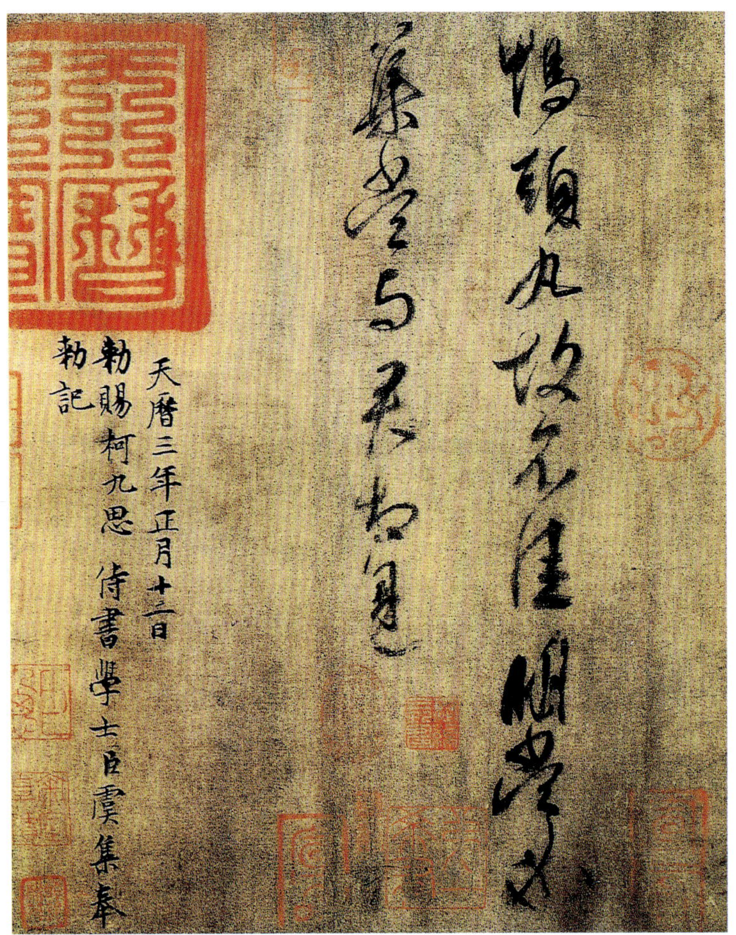

Figure 4
***Letter about Duck's Head Pill* (鸭头丸帖, *Ya Tou Wan Tie*)**
Wang Xianzhi (344 – 386, Eastern Jin Dynasty)
Semi-cursive script
26.1 cm × 26.9 cm
Shanghai Museum

Letter about Duck's Head Pill is a short letter Wang Xianzhi wrote to his friend or relative. It consists of fifteen characters in two lines, which translates to "The duck's head pill (a kind of Chinese medicine) is ineffective. I will meet with you tomorrow at the gathering to discuss about this."

All the 15 characters are linked with one another from top to bottom, hence the designation of "one brush stroke calligraphic work." However, this does not mean that the work is completed in a single brush stroke. It is in fact a description of the great momentum exhibited all through this work. Completed in one go, the characters, though not entirely linked with each other, fully display the calligrapher's coherence in thought. With a distinctive yet balanced use of ink, the work looks rhythmic and natural.

achieved remained unsurpassed even today. It was they who determined the direction of semi-cursive script development, pushed its artistic expression to the extreme, and demonstrated the essence of Chinese calligraphic art to the fullest.

The Tang Dynasty: Period of Prosperity

The second big leap in the history of semi-cursive script lasted from the mid-Tang Dynasty (618 – 907) to the Song Dynasty (960 – 1279), when all of society, from the ruling class to men of letters and scholar officials, held calligraphy in high esteem. Against this background emerged a group of calligraphers of great individuality who were well versed in running-cursive script, the most representative of whom were Yan Zhenqing (709 – 785) of the Tang Dynasty and Su Shi, Huang Tingjian (1045 – 1105), and Mi Fu (1051 – 1107) of the Song Dynasty.

The Tang Dynasty was another period of calligraphic prosperity as a result of the thriving civil service examination where the standardized regular script became popular at that time. Meanwhile, the rulers' love of calligraphy also promoted the tremendous development of seal script, clerical script, cursive script, and semi-cursive script. This period witnessed the emergence of a large group of calligraphers adept at different scripts from among emperors, officials, poets, and monks. Yan Zhenqing was one of the most outstanding of them all.

Yan served four emperors in succession. He was a prestigious, high-ranking scholar-official

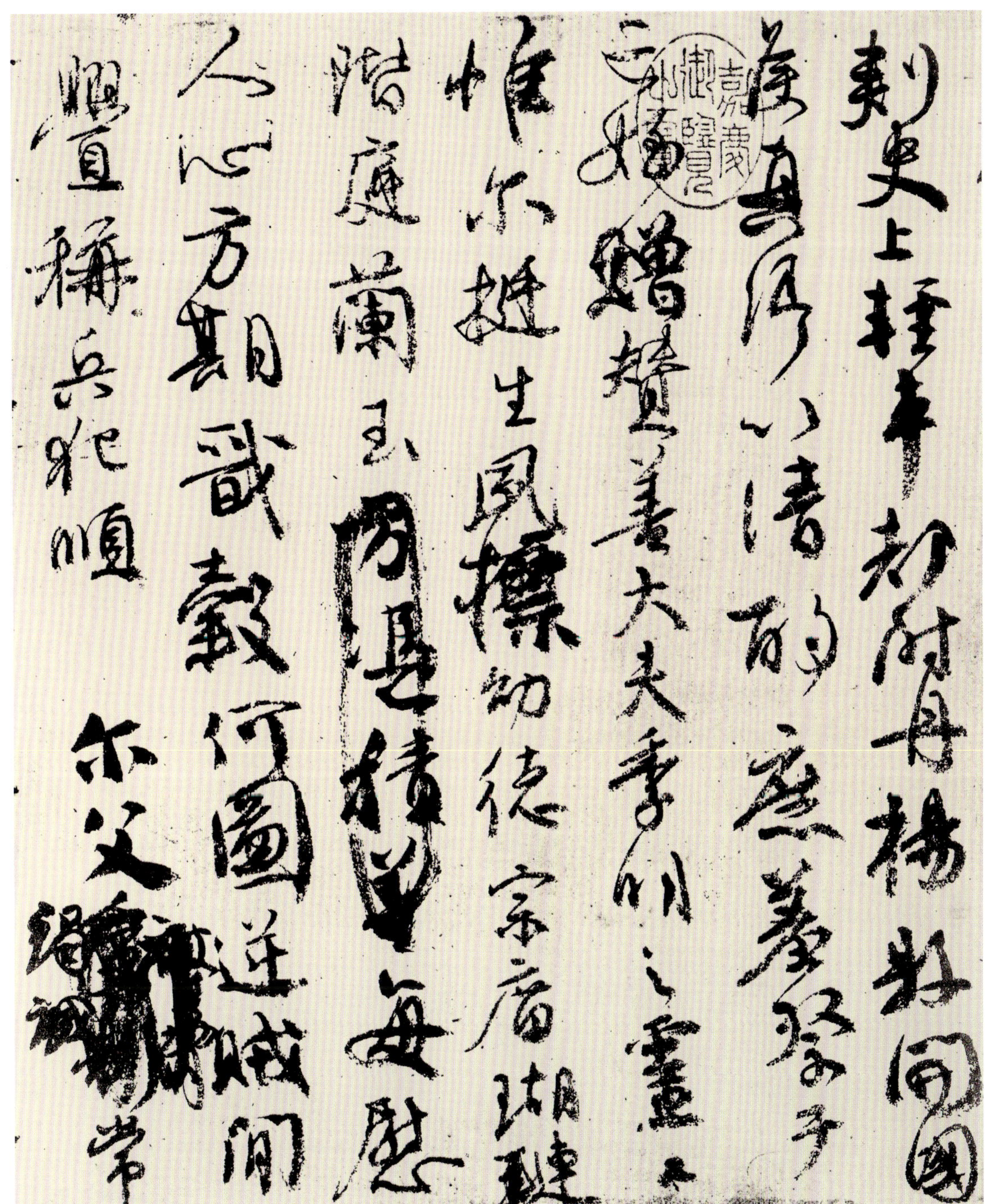

Figure 5
Draft Eulogy for a Nephew (祭侄文稿, *Ji Zhi Wen Gao*)
Yan Zhenqing (708 – 784, Tang Dynasty)
Semi-cursive script
28.2 cm × 75.5 cm
Palace Museum, Taipei

Draft Eulogy for a Nephew, the most famous calligraphic work in semi-cursive script by Yan Zhenqing, is an authentic depiction of the calligrapher's personality. He composed this masterpiece in a grievous and indignant mood upon hearing the news that Yan Jimin, his nephew, had been killed by the rebellious army. The work, completed in one go, is characterized by changing dots and strokes and a fine integration of the calligrapher's strong emotions and superb calligraphic skills, displaying his great grief and indignation and producing an extremely strong visual impact. It is known as "the world's second best semi-cursive script."

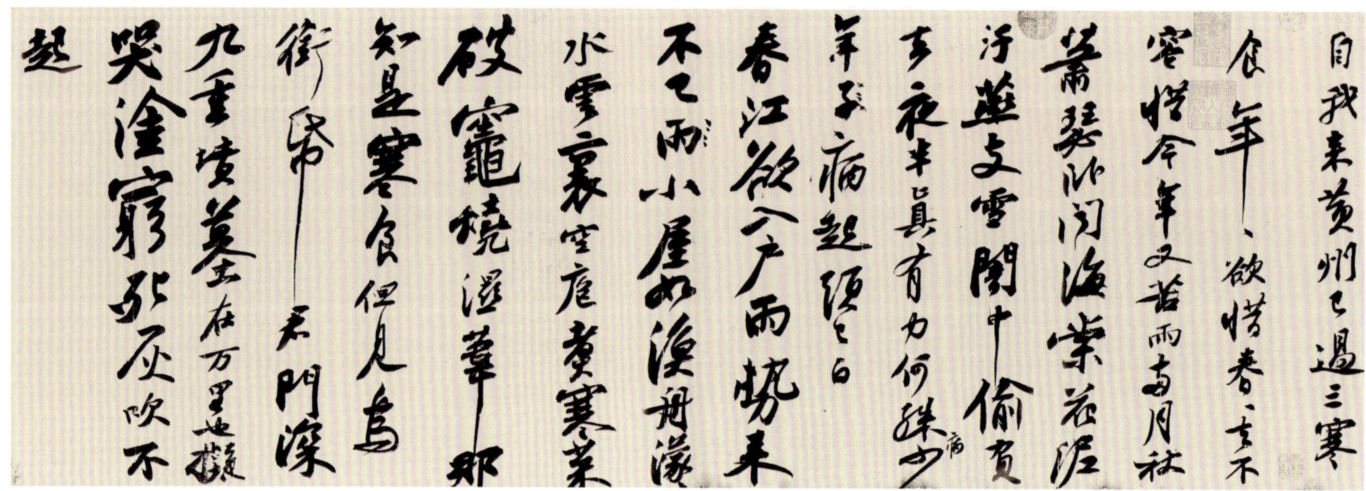

with an upright and unyielding character. He was versatile in calligraphy, particularly adept at regular and semi-cursive scripts, and his calligraphic style was known as the "Yan-style calligraphy" (Figure 5). The semi-cursive script of Yan Zhenqing revealed his profound foundation in calligraphy resulting from his many years of study of his predecessors' calligraphic experience. What's more noticeable was that his calligraphy fully displayed his broad-mindedness and sense of righteousness, a fine proof of the Chinese saying "the handwriting reveals the writer." The Yan-style regular and semi-cursive scripts had an influence on later generations second only to those of Wang Xizhi and Wang Xianzhi.

If the Wei and Jin periods are taken as the romantic age of Chinese calligraphy and the Tang Dynasty the realistic age, then the Song Dynasty is the age of rationalism. Influenced by the political and social turbulence and the philosophical and religious concepts of that time, calligraphers in the Song Dynasty focused more on calligraphic

Figure 6
***Poem to Express Melancholy after Demotion* (黄州寒食诗卷, *Huang Zhou Han Shi Shi Juan*)**
Su Shi (1037 – 1101, Song Dynasty)
Semi-cursive script
33.5 cm × 118 cm
Palace Museum, Taipei

Connoisseurs from different times have shown great admiration for this work by Su Shi, which is known as "the world's third best semi-cursive script." This calligraphic work, having no inscriptions and date of creation on it, was composed and written in 1082, the 5th year of Emperor Zhao Xu's reign in the Northern Song Dynasty, when the calligrapher was banished to the remote and frontier Huangzhou for a nominal post, due to his criticism of the reformist faction at court. Feeling lonely and abandoned in spirit and being reduced to extreme poverty, he composed two bleak poems with five characters to each line at the Cold Food Festival (falling upon April 3 or 4) three years after his arrival in Huangzhou to express his disconsolations.

Overall, this work is a fine display of the calligrapher's bold and unrestrained calligraphic style, the characters looking steep but steady, full of passion, force, and momentum. They are written in an unusually rugged and unrestrained manner, not big or small, dense or loose, presenting a picturesque disorder in a myriad of changes.

knowledge accumulation and self-cultivation. The semi-cursive script naturally became one of the best means for them to escape reality and display individuality.

The Song Dynasty witnessed the emergence of the most famous calligrapher group in history, known as "The Big Four," including Su Shi, Huang Tingjian, Mi Fu, and Cai Xiang (1012 – 1067). The four of them, like teacher and friend, had all made remarkable achievements in essays, poetry, calligraphy, and painting. Learning from the ancients and being innovative, they had formed a calligraphic style of their own, gaining immense admiration from later generations. Of the four, the previous three were the most outstanding.

Though they were all excellent calligraphers of that time, they exhibited sharply different styles of semi-cursive script due to their differences in personality and aesthetic pursuits. Opinions differ as to which of them was the best. For many people, Su Shi should rank first indisputably, since as a master calligrapher noted for a style that was mellow and rigorous, innocent and care-free, bold and unrestrained, natural and unembellished, he led the new calligraphic style prevalent in the Song Dynasty, a style that emphasized the expression of the calligrapher's personal feelings and emotions through calligraphy and, in particular, a free mentality in calligraphic production (Figure 6).

Naturally, there are also admirers of Huang Tingjian who insist that Huang was the most innovative of the four, as his works were elegantly imposing and original, showing the calligrapher's effort to innovate. However, it was Mi Fu and his works that exerted the greatest influence on calligraphers of later generations. For all his life, Mi Fu had been in pursuit of an extraordinarily refined calligraphic style. Learning from and imitating the ancients, he finally formed his own bold and unrestrained style and reached the highest attainment in semi-cursive script.

Innovations in printing technology have made it possible to preserve many of the authentic works of the four calligraphers, elevating their influence on modern Chinese calligraphy above their predecessors. Quite a number of later calligraphers were nurtured by calligraphers of this time, such as Zhao Mengfu and Xianyu Shu (1256 – 1301) in the Yuan Dynasty and Zhu Yunming (1460 – 1527), Xu Wei (1521 – 1593), and Dong Qichang (1555 – 1636) in the Ming Dynasty. Each of them boasted his own calligraphic style, either refined and graceful or bold and unrestrained.

The Ming and Qing Dynasties: Returning to Simplicity

From the late Ming Dynasty (1368 – 1644) to the Qing Dynasty (1644 – 1911), semi-cursive script completed its third leap in development.

First, a group of calligraphers who were well versed in running-cursive script and who emphasized the calligraphic form emerged in the late Ming Dynasty, such as Wang Duo (1592 – 1652) (Figure 7), Fu Shan (1607 – 1684), and Zheng Xie (1693 – 1765). Their works of semi-cursive script boasted vivid and highly individualized styles, presenting great momentum, not bothering about trifles, and pursuing exaggerated visual effects. Second, in the late Qing Dynasty, an enthusiasm for stone

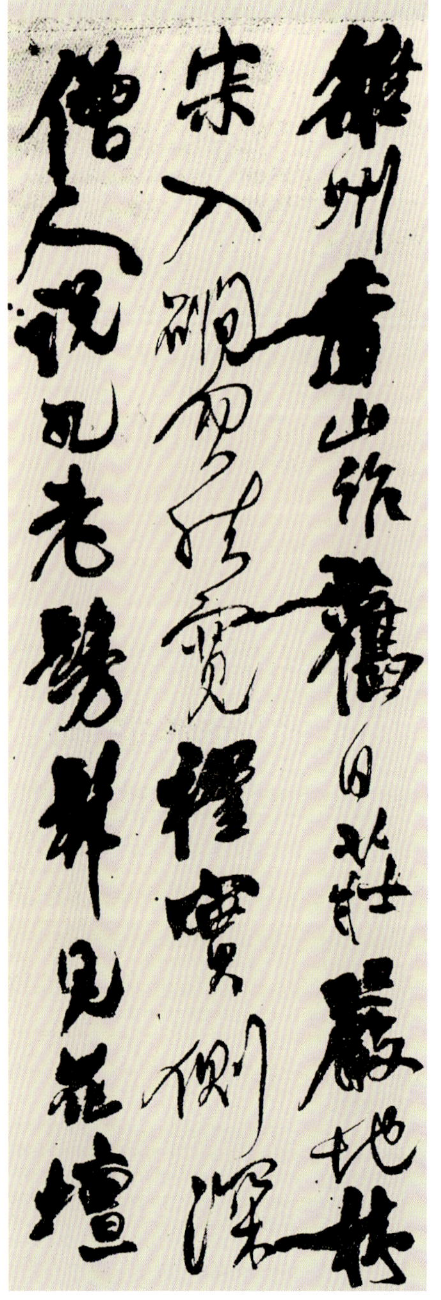

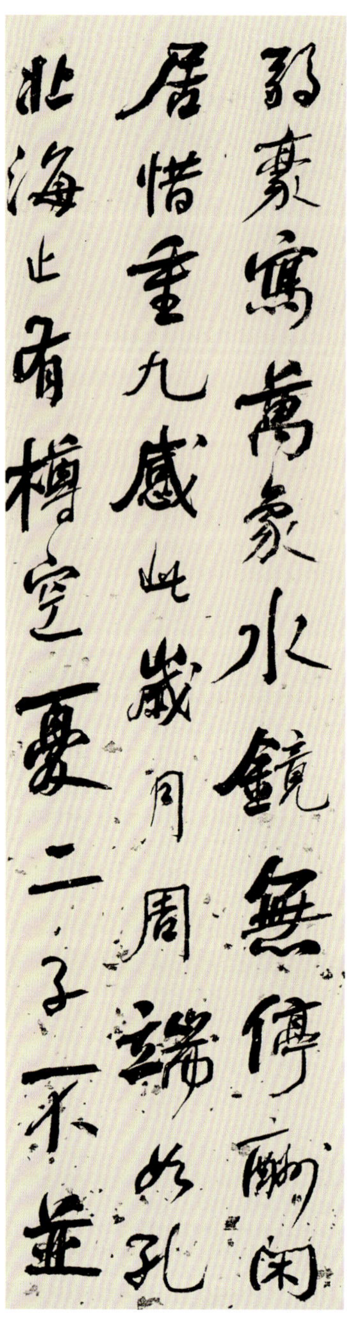

Figure 7 (*far left*)
Poem about Mount Xiang **(雒州香山作, *Luo Zhou Xiang Shan Zuo*)**
Wang Duo (1592 – 1652, Ming Dynasty)
Semi-cursive script

Wang Duo, a minister in the late Ming and early Qing dynasties, is an expert of calligraphy and painting. This work is characterized by fluent dots and strokes, an expert use of ink, a perfect combination of thick and thin strokes, and a proportional utilization of dry and moist brush techniques. Though grotesque in shape and slanted, the characters are coherent in spirit and look like an organic whole. The overall composition of this work is energetic, bold, and unrestrained, producing an extremely strong visual impact.

Figure 8 (*left*)
Su Shi's Poems in Reply to Tao Yuanming's Poems **(东坡和陶诗, *Dong Po He Tao Shi*)**
He Shaoji (1799 – 1873, Qing Dynasty)
Semi-cursive script

Su Shi had the greatest admiration for Tao Yuanming's poems and composed a large number of poems after Tao's poetic style, which are were known as "poems in reply to Tao Yuanming's poems." For all his life, Su Shi had dreamed of living a life of a hermit as Tao Yuanming did, but without success.

He Shaoji was a poet, painter, and calligrapher in the late Qing Dynasty. His calligraphic work, *Su Shi's Poems in Reply to Tao Yuanming's Poems*, consists of characters with round, plump strokes, written in a primitive and crude manner, yet showing great strength. The characters are generally outreaching to the left, showing the calligrapher's sole focus on steadiness and robustness, instead of on the characters' postures. Moreover, the calligrapher has integrated the structural characteristics of seal and clerical scripts into his running-cursive script, producing works of immense admiration.

tablet calligraphy began to arise. Calligraphers were devoted to researching the calligraphy carved on ancient stone tablets and tombstones, and as a result, the solid and compact style of stone tablet calligraphy was gradually integrated into the flowing running-cursive script, rendering it with a new outlook of simplicity and vigor. Some of the outstanding calligraphers of that time, such as He Shaoji (1799 – 1833) (Figure 8), Zhao Zhiqian (1829 – 1884) (Figure 9), and Shen Zengzhi (1850 – 1922), still have their impact felt today.

Semi-cursive script, a popular form of handwriting with artistic and practical values, has survived the vicissitudes of time to live on until today. It is bound to have a brighter future tomorrow.

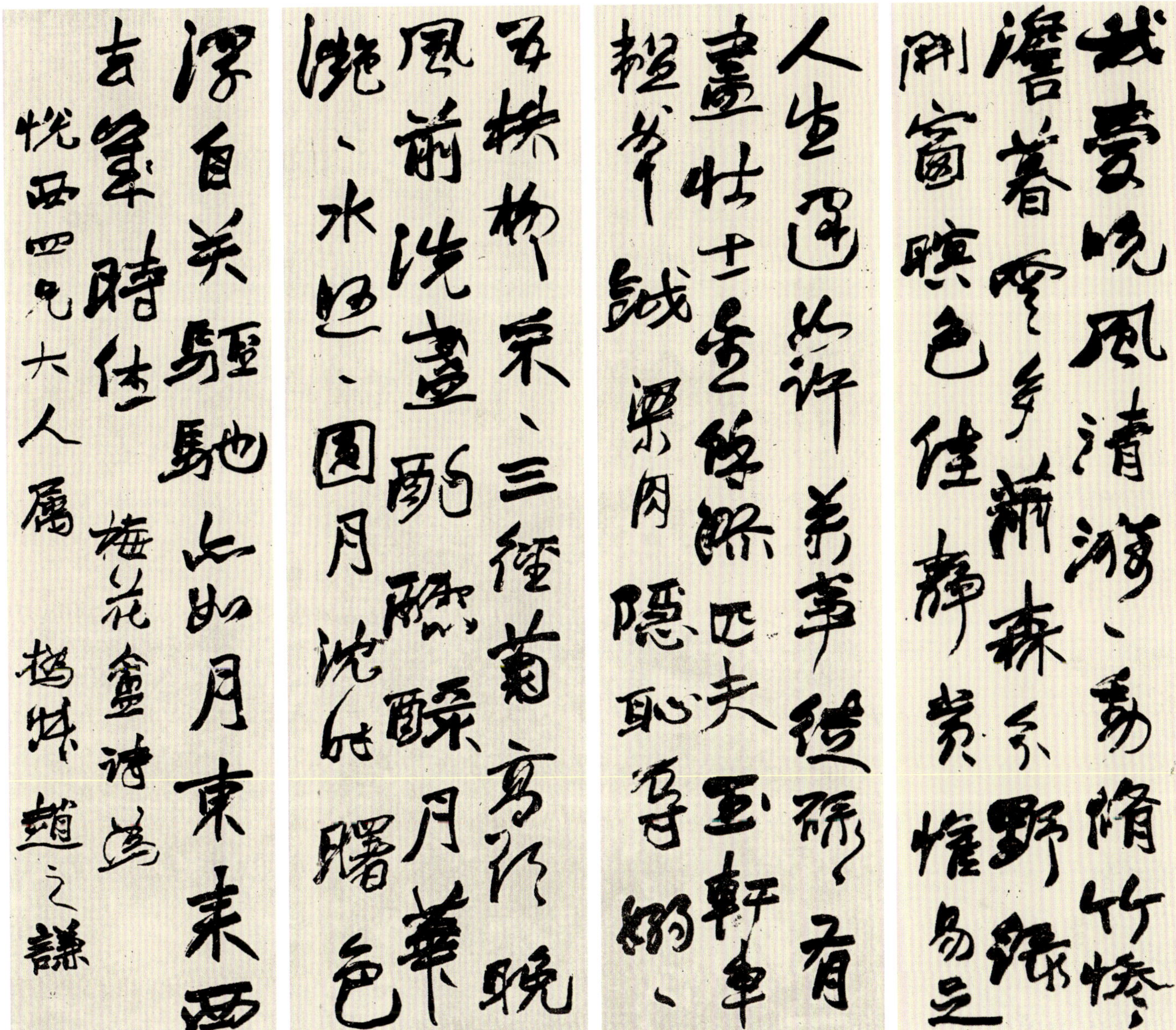

Figure 9
Plum Blossom Hut **(梅花庵诗, *Mei Hua An Shi*)**
Zhao Zhiqian (1829 – 1884, Qing Dynasty)
Semi-cursive script

Zhao Zhiqian was the most famous painter, calligrapher, and seal-carving artist in the late Qing Dynasty. Following the artistic style popular in the Qin and Han dynasties, he created his own unique style based on a thorough understanding of seal, clerical, and semi-cursive scripts.

The characters in *Plum Blossom Hut* are slant and oblate, squeezing each other from the top. The adoption of the distinctive calligraphic techniques typical of the Northern Wei Dynasty (386 – 557) renders the work solid and stocky. This work exhibits a unique art of composition, with big and small characters in picturesque disorder and lines interwoven with each other, reminding the viewers of the poetic line "pearls, big and small, falling into a jade plate."

3. Artistic Features and Values of Semi-Cursive Script

With a history of over 1,800 years, semi-cursive script is favored by artists and men of letters whether in artistic creation or in daily life. Specifically, three important features have contributed to its long-term prosperity.

Unrestricted Rules of Writing

From its start in the Eastern Han Dynasty to the birth of *Preface to the Orchid Pavilion Collection* by Wang Xizhi in 353, semi-cursive script reached its first peak of development in no more than 150 years, which was completely attributed to its extremely unrestricted rules of writing. Unlike clerical, regular, and cursive scripts, semi-cursive script does not have a set of standardized and systematic writing rules for calligraphers to follow.

It can be regarded as a calligraphic style through which cursive script evolves to regular script, or a medium style that consists of running-regular script (*xingkaishu*) and running-cursive script. The former, though somewhat regular, is written much faster, with obviously colluding strokes, as is evidenced in *Preface to the Orchid Pavilion Collection*. The latter is closer to cursive script, bolder and more unrestrained in style and with more colluding strokes, as is shown in *Letter about Duck's Head Pill* by Wang Xianzhi.

Compared with regular script, semi-cursive script is simpler and faster in writing; compared with cursive script, semi-cursive script is easier to recognize. All these allow this script a relatively freer space of writing and make it one of the most popular scripts.

High Degree of Integration

In the process of independent development and self-improvement, seal script, clerical script, regular script, and cursive script have each formed a relatively closed pattern of development, as each of them boasts a set of complete and systematic rules of writing. However, semi-cursive script is an exception.

Judging from the calligraphic works of different dynasties, semi-cursive script can always move among different scripts with great ease and set each other off perfectly, forming a distinctive style of writing in the end. For example, *Letter to a Relative* (伯远帖, *Bo Yuan Tie*) by Wang Xun (349 – 400), *Rhyme Prose* (文赋帖, *Wen Fu Tie*) by Lu Jianzhi (585 – 638), and *General Pei Poetry* (裴将军诗帖, *Pei Jiang Jun Shi Tie*) by Yan Zhenqing are all models of calligraphic works that integrate cursive, semi-cursive, and regular scripts into a whole. This high degree of integration enabled semi-cursive script to flourish all the way to now.

High Degree of Popularity

Though semi-cursive script has stroke connections and omissions, it uses few or no special symbols and keeps the orthographic structure of Chinese characters in more places. Therefore, either the semi-cursive calligraphic works of Wang Xizhi and Wang Xianzhi or those of Zhao Mengfu and Dong Qichang

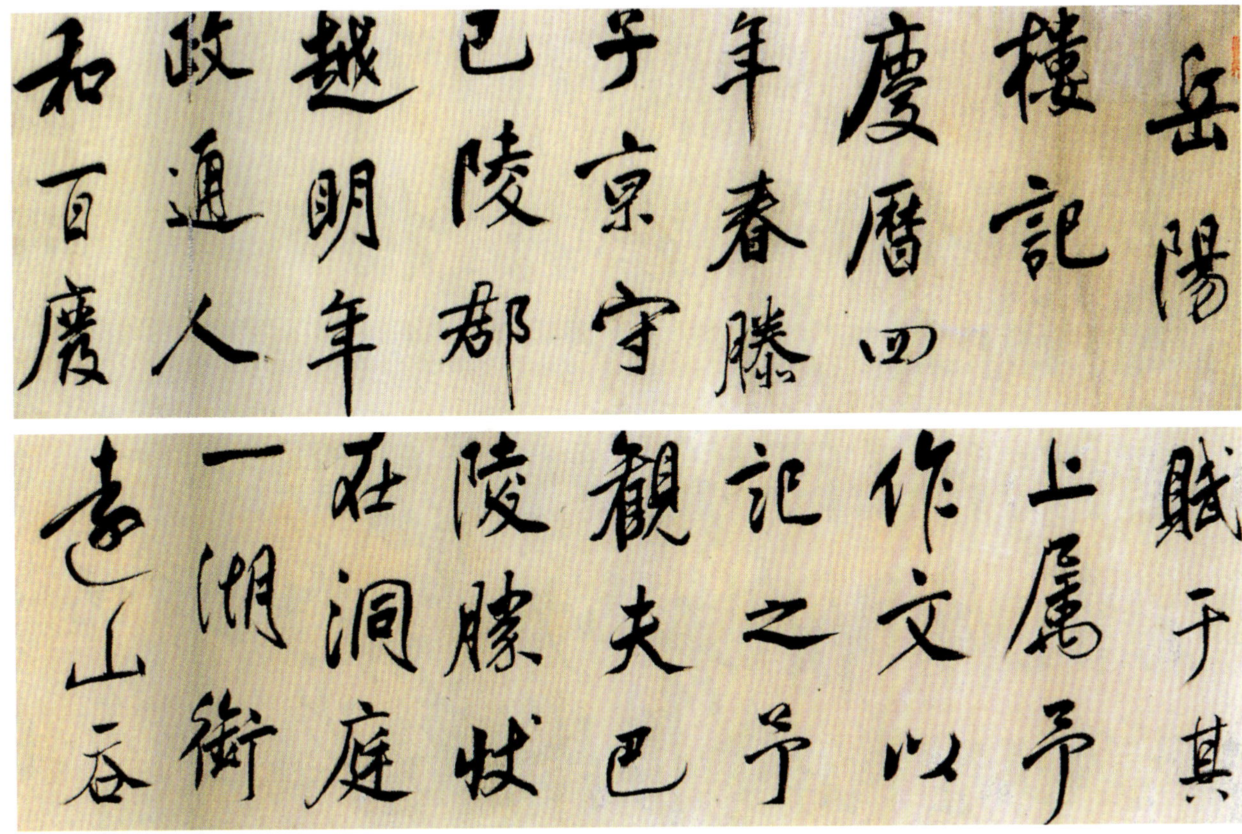

Figure 10
Yueyang Pavilion **(岳阳楼记, *Yue Yang Lou Ji*)**
Dong Qichang (1555 – 1636, Ming Dynasty)
Semi-cursive script
37.6 cm × 1499.5 cm
Palace Museum, Beijing

Dong Qichang was exceptionally gifted and quick witted. He was familiar with Zen Buddhism, good at appreciation and collection, and well versed in poetry, painting, and painting theories. An exceptional and influential calligrapher and painter in the late Ming Dynasty, he had achieved the highest attainment in semi-cursive and cursive scripts.

Yueyang Pavilion, a long scroll of semi-cursive script, is among the best of Dong Qichang's works. This work, a record of the highly renowned essay *Yueyang Pavalion* by Fan Zhongyan (989 – 1052) of the Northern Song Dynasty, was written in 1609, when Dong was 55 years of age and remained idle at home for four months before taking up a new post. During that time, struggles between different political parties and schools at the royal court had grown in intensity and Dong wrote this essay to show his repugnance to this trend.

Based on lofty concepts, this work is facile and graceful, striking a perfect balance between effort and ease, and presenting a charm unique to it. The strokes are simple and elegant, showing strength and ease. In character composition, Dong Qichang pursues order within disorder, seeming to follow Yang Ningshi (873 – 954), an influential calligrapher in the Tang Dynasty. The characters and lines in his works are evenly scattered, showing the calligrapher's effort to pursue the ancient calligraphic tradition.

(Figure 10) are easy to recognize and imitate. Although semi-cursive script has undergone several changes in style during its development, it still strives to suit both refined and popular tastes.

Today, it is quite rare for people to write with a writing brush in their daily lives; however, most of their handwritings written with hard-tipped writing instruments are in semi-cursive script. This proves that semi-cursive script remains a writing style that keeps pace with the change of time and that best expresses the writer's inner feelings and emotions.

The free and compatible style of semi-cursive script has aroused the creative passion of many calligraphers, giving birth to a large number of distinctive masters of calligraphy, such as Wang Xizhi, Wang Xianzhi, Yan Zhenqing, Su Shi, Mi Fu, Zhao Mengfu, and Dong Qichang, and to a galaxy of masterpieces, all of which have become the most cherished items in the treasure house of Chinese calligraphic art.

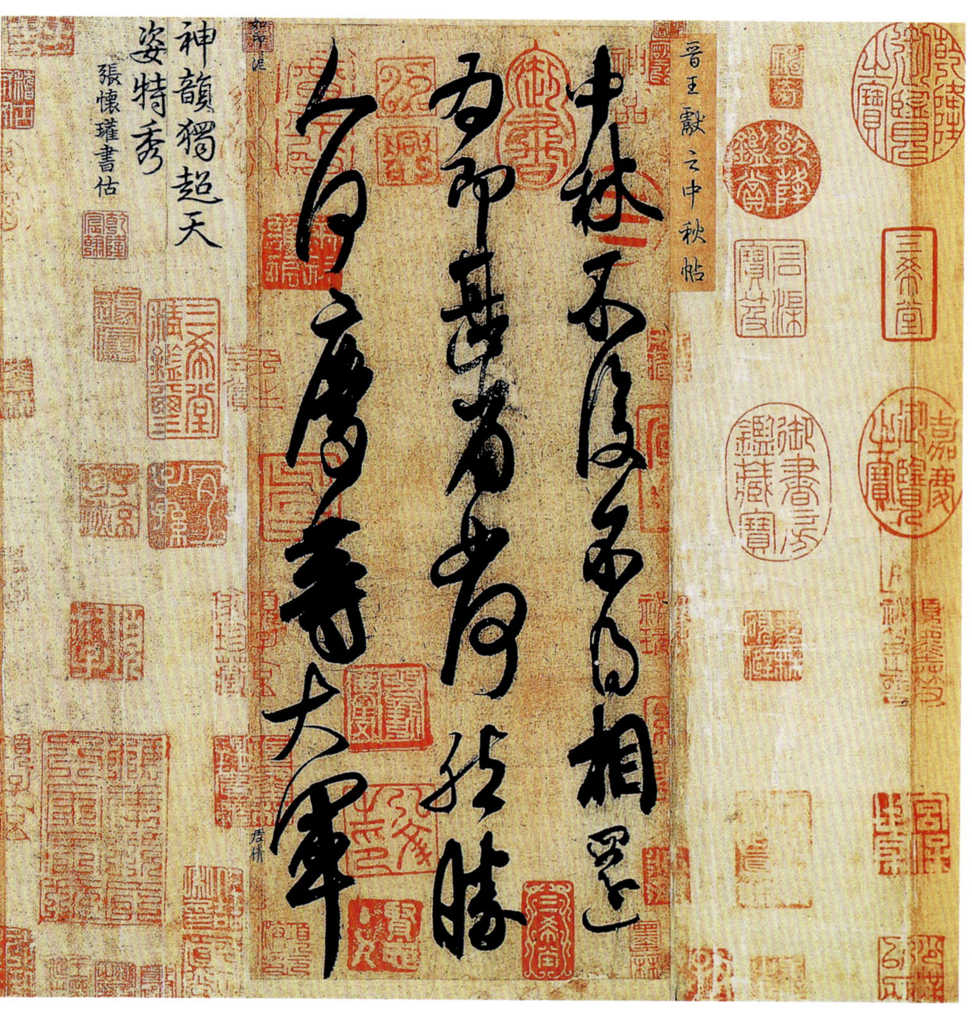

4. Masterpieces of Semi-Cursive Script across Dynasties

It is by no means easy to choose representative works of semi-cursive script from among the vast number of masterpieces from ancient time to today. However, this book has a selection of works from ten calligraphers, whose reputation has been unmatched in the history of Chinese semi-cursive script. More importantly, each of these works has been indisputably considered as the example of its time, through which the development of semi-cursive script has been revealed.

Mid-Autumn Scroll (中秋帖, *Zhong Qiu Tie*)
Wang Xianzhi (344 – 386, Eastern Jin Dynasty)
Semi-cursive script
27 cm × 11.9 cm
Palace Museum, Beijing

This work, together with *Letter to Express Happiness and Greetings* (快雪时晴帖, *Kuai xue Shi Qing Tie*), a masterpiece of Wang Xizhi, father of Wang Xianzhi, is taken as one of the three rare calligraphic treasures. Produced without a stop and in a free and unrestrained manner, it is known as a "one brush stroke calligraphic work." The work, a paragon of semi-cursive script, is a fine model for calligraphy learners.

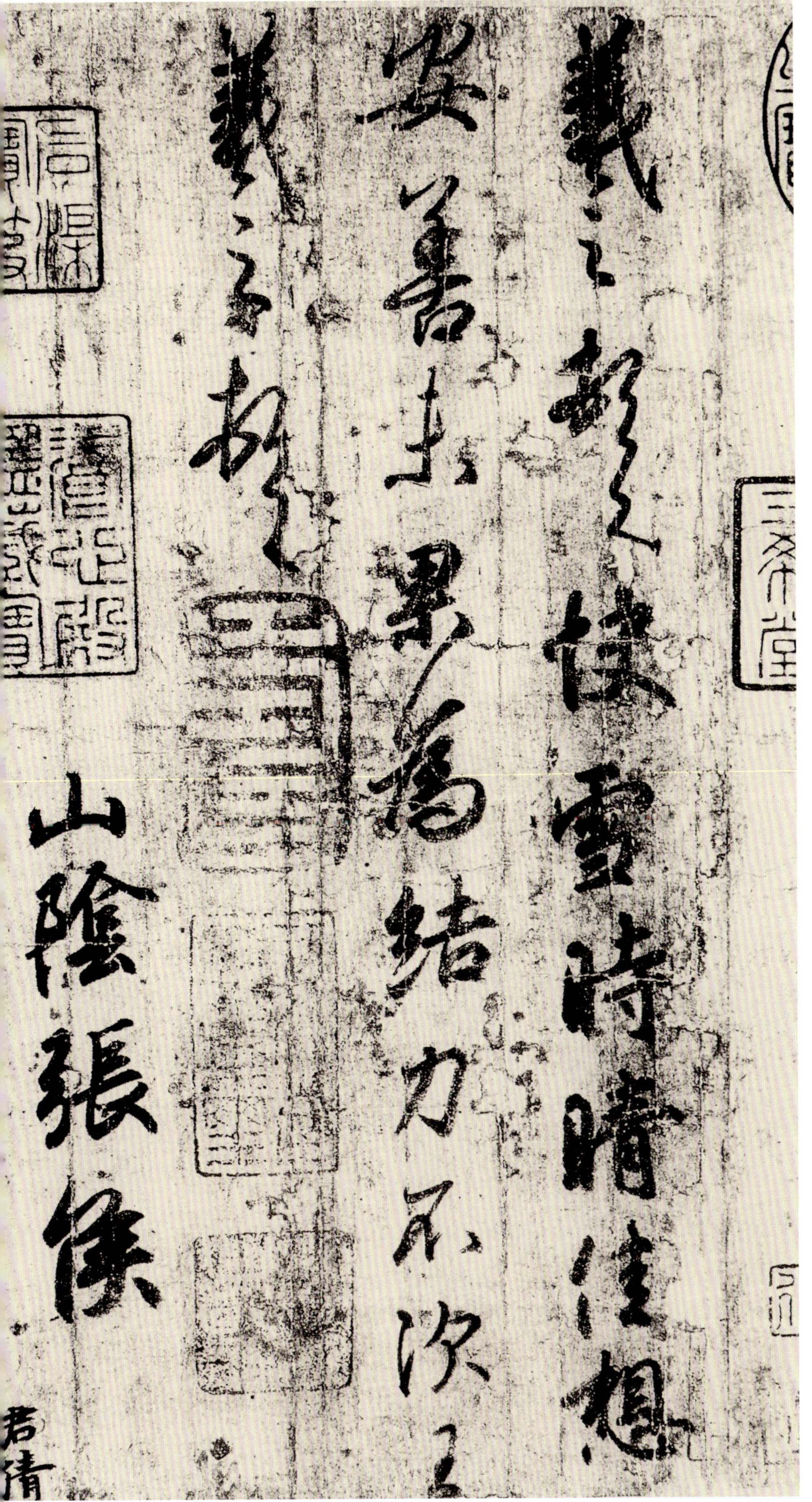

Letter to Express Happiness and Greetings (快雪时晴帖, *Kuai Xue Shi Qing Tie*)
Wang Xizhi (303 – 361, or 321 – 379 according to some sources, Eastern Jin Dynasty)
Semi-cursive script
32 cm × 14.8 cm
Palace Museum, Taipei

This work, consisting of 28 characters in 4 lines, records the calligrapher's light-hearted mood when the sky cleared up after a heavy snow and his greetings to his relatives and friends. Having integrated the techniques of regular script, it looks fluent and smooth, elegant and beautiful. The strokes are mellow and full and do not expose themselves, a fine display of the calligrapher's consistent writing style of flowing and harmonious beauty. This work, together with Wang Xun's *Letter to a Relative* and Wang Xianzhi's *Mid-Autumn Scroll*, was once stored in Sanxi Hall (Hall of Three Rare Calligraphic Treasures) of Imperial Palace by Emperor Qianlong of the Qing Dynasty, demonstrating its value as a rare calligraphic treasure.

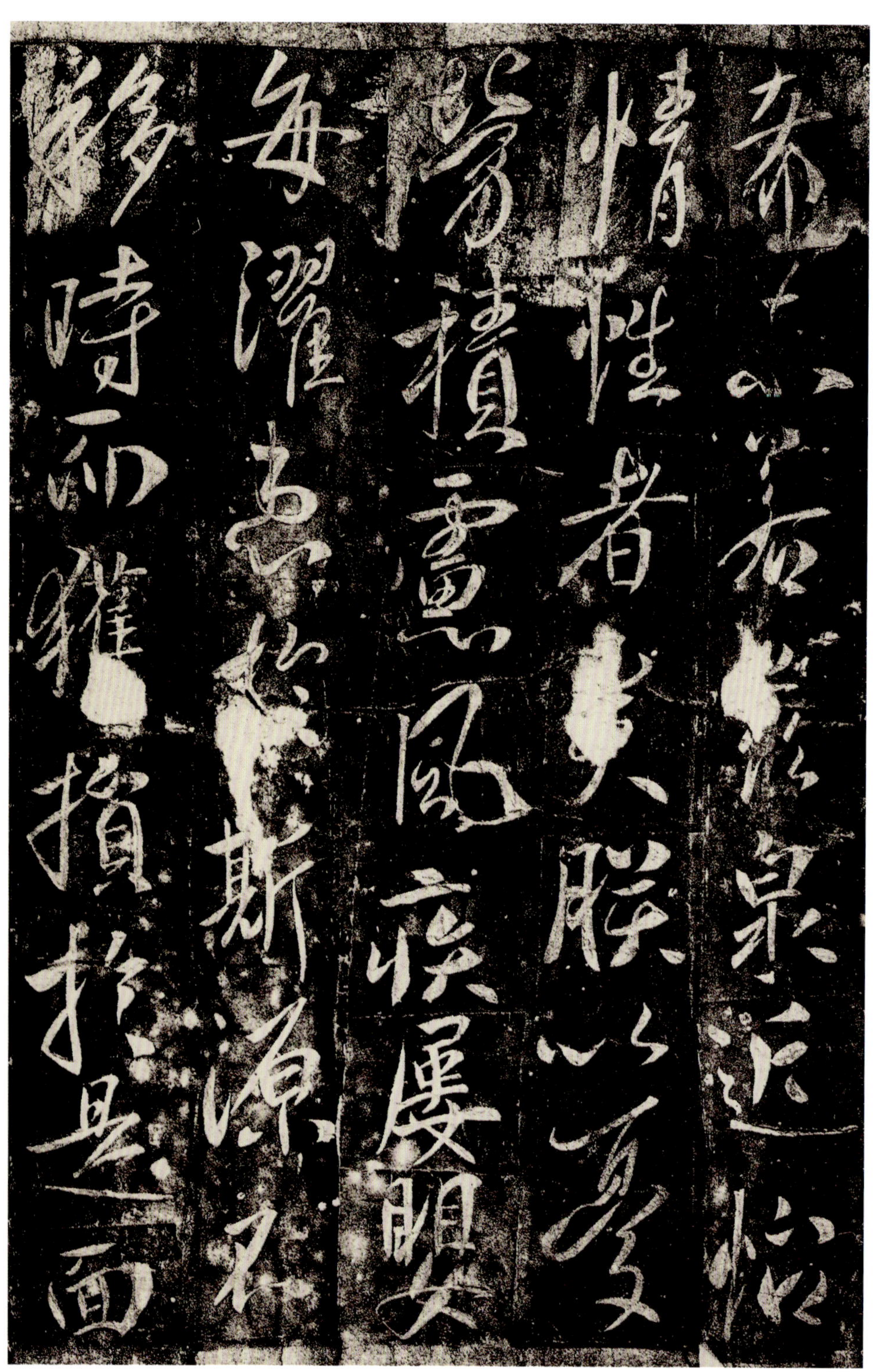

Spring (温泉铭, *Wen Quan Ming*)
Li Shimin (599 – 649, Tang Dynasty)
Semi-cursive script
Bibliothèque Nationale de France, Paris

Though he was an emperor, Li Shimin was extremely accomplished in calligraphic theory and practice, following the semi-cursive script of Wang Xizhi in the main. This work, completed in his later years for the Spring in Mount Li in what is now Xi'an today, exhibits vivid brush styles, ever-changing character postures, and overall, the calligrapher's superb command of calligraphic skills.

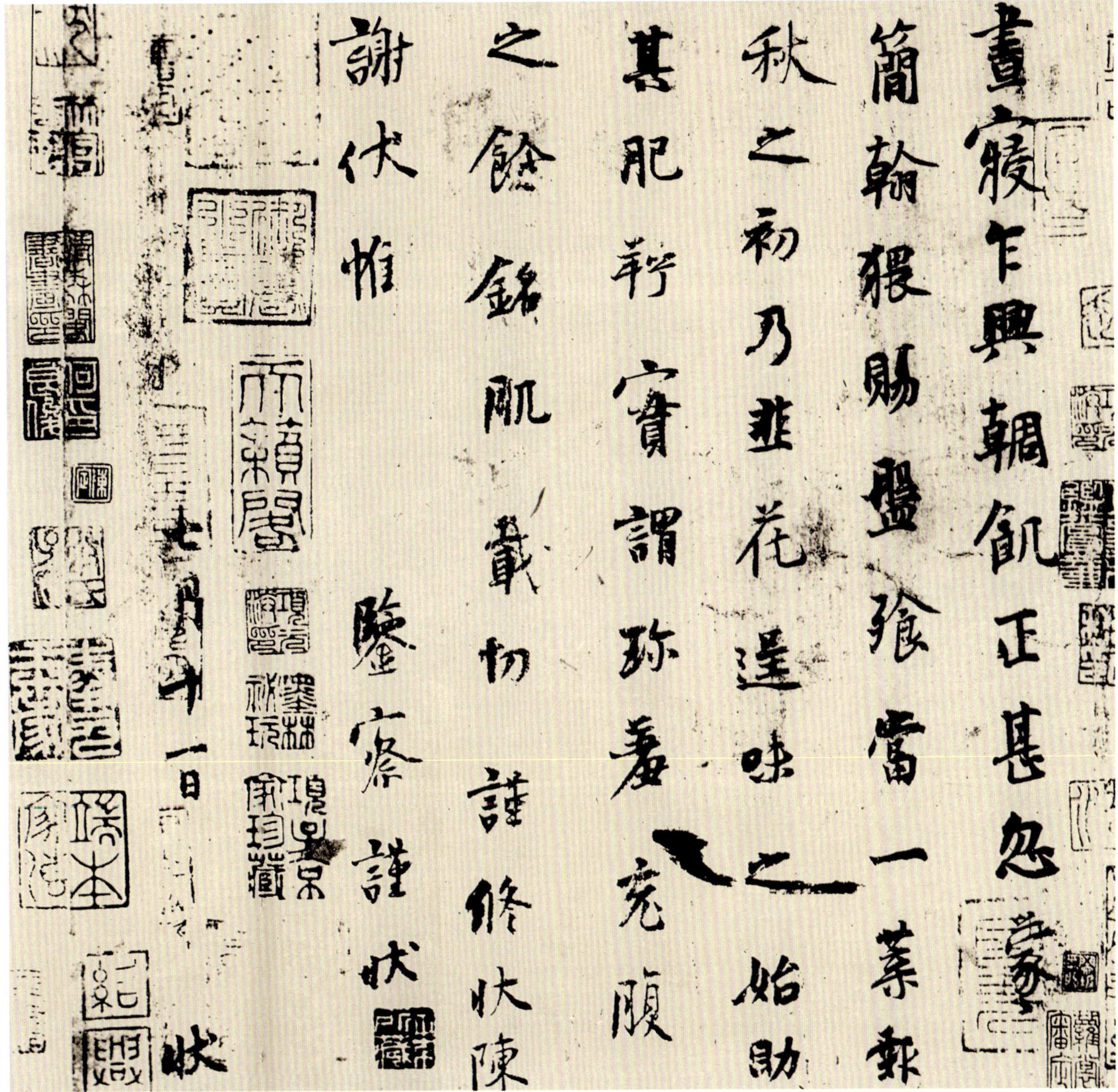

A Gift of Chives (韭花帖, *Jiu Hua Tie*)
Yang Ningshi (873 – 954, Tang Dynasty)
Running-regular script
26 cm × 28 cm
Lanqianshan Museum of Taiwan; Office of Culture of the Municipality of Wuxi

This work is a letter of 63 characters in 7 lines. It records such a scene: The calligrapher, waking up from an afternoon nap, feels hungry. Just then, someone brings delicious chives to him. He then gladly wrote this piece to express his gratitude. This work is between semi-cursive script and regular script in style, with a wandering and unfolding layout and graceful characters. It is a model work of semi-cursive script, winning widespread admiration of scholars of later generations.

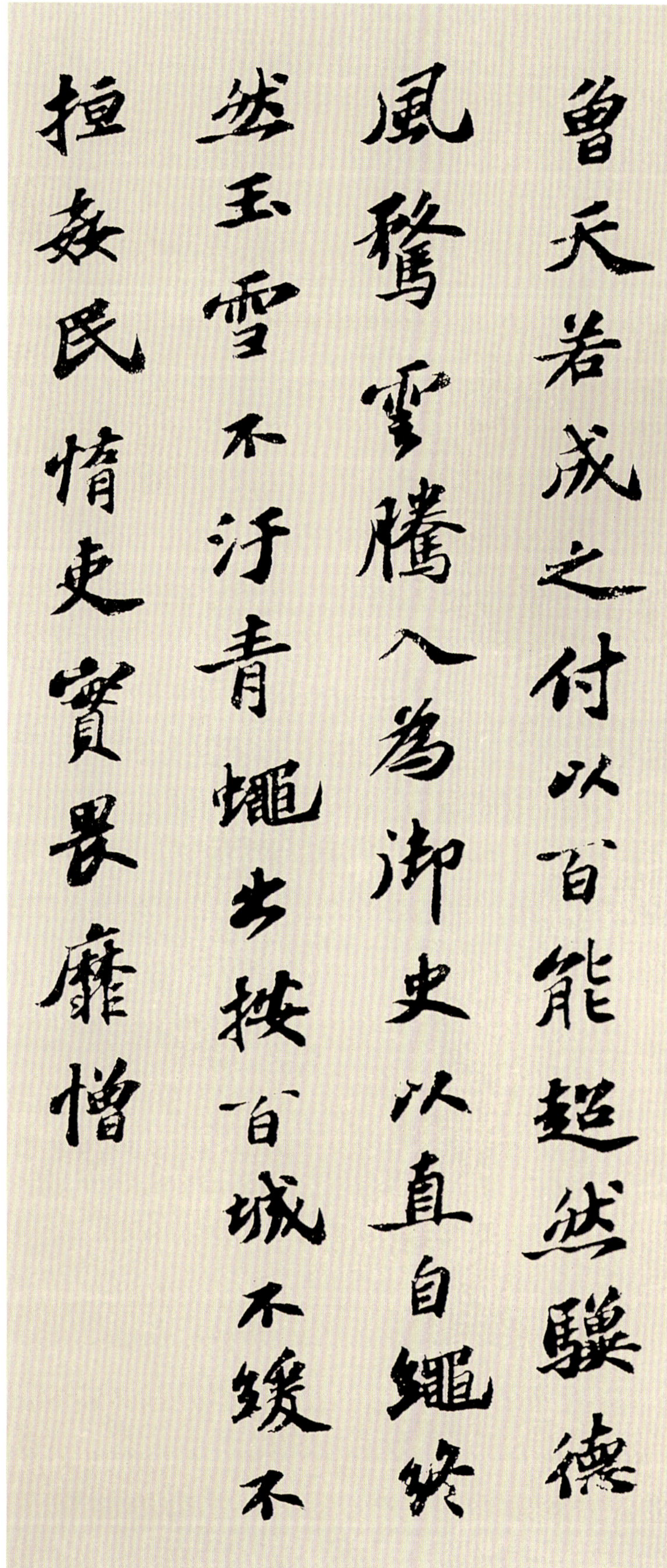

In Memory of Huang Jidao (祭黄几道文, *Ji Huang Ji Dao Wen*)
Su Shi (1037 – 1101, Song Dynasty)
Running-regular script
31.6 cm × 121.7 cm
Shanghai Museum

This work was composed by the calligrapher at the age of fifty-two to mourn the passing of his friend Huang Jidao. A model of calligraphy, it blends the style of semi-cursive script into that of regular script, displaying a natural and innocent style filled with traditional simplicity. It is one of the very few works of the calligrapher that have been passed down.

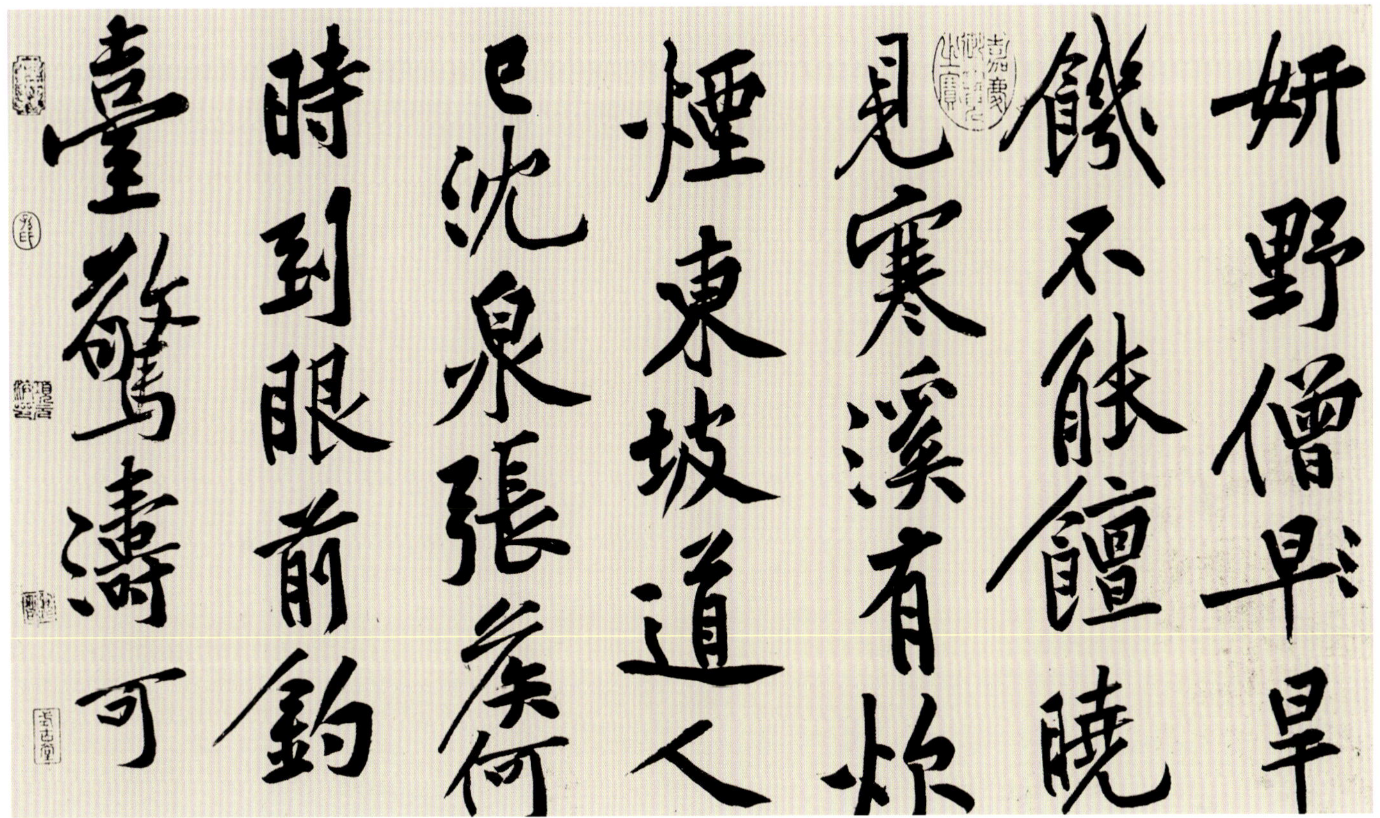

Poem on Pine Pavilion (松风阁诗, *Song Feng Ge Shi*)
Huang Tingjian (1045 – 1105, Song Dynasty)
Semi-cursive script
Palace Museum, Taipei

Pine Pavilion is close to Lingquan Temple in Hubei province. The calligrapher once traveled there with his friends and, astonished by the natural scenery, composed this masterpiece. Huang's work of semi-cursive script is natural, simple and vigorous. This work is a representative work of his semi-cursive script.

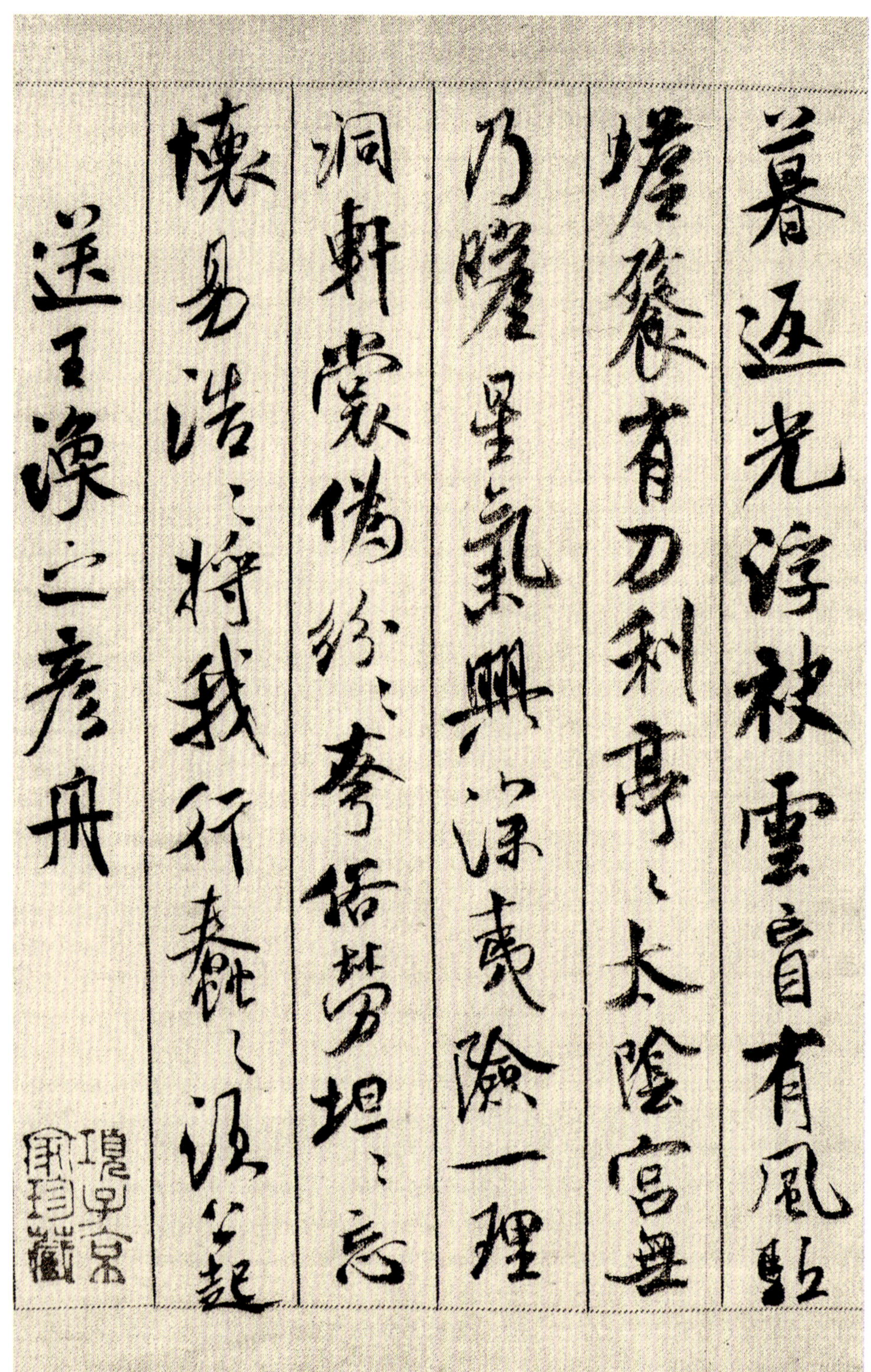

Poems Written on Sichuan Silk (蜀素帖, *Shu Su Tie*)
Mi Fu (1051 – 1107, Song Dynasty)
Semi-cursive script
29.7 cm ×284.3 cm
Palace Museum, Taipei

Mi Fu was one of the most outstanding calligraphers versed in semi-cursive script in the Song Dynasty. He was well educated and good at adopting advice from his peers, gradually developing a style of his own. Sichuan silk was of fine quality then. Since Mi Fu wrote his eight poems on this kind of silk, the work was named *Poems Written on Sichuan Silk*, which is representative of the calligrapher's works. With a multitude of graceful stroke changes, this work shows a dynamic beauty unique to the calligrapher.

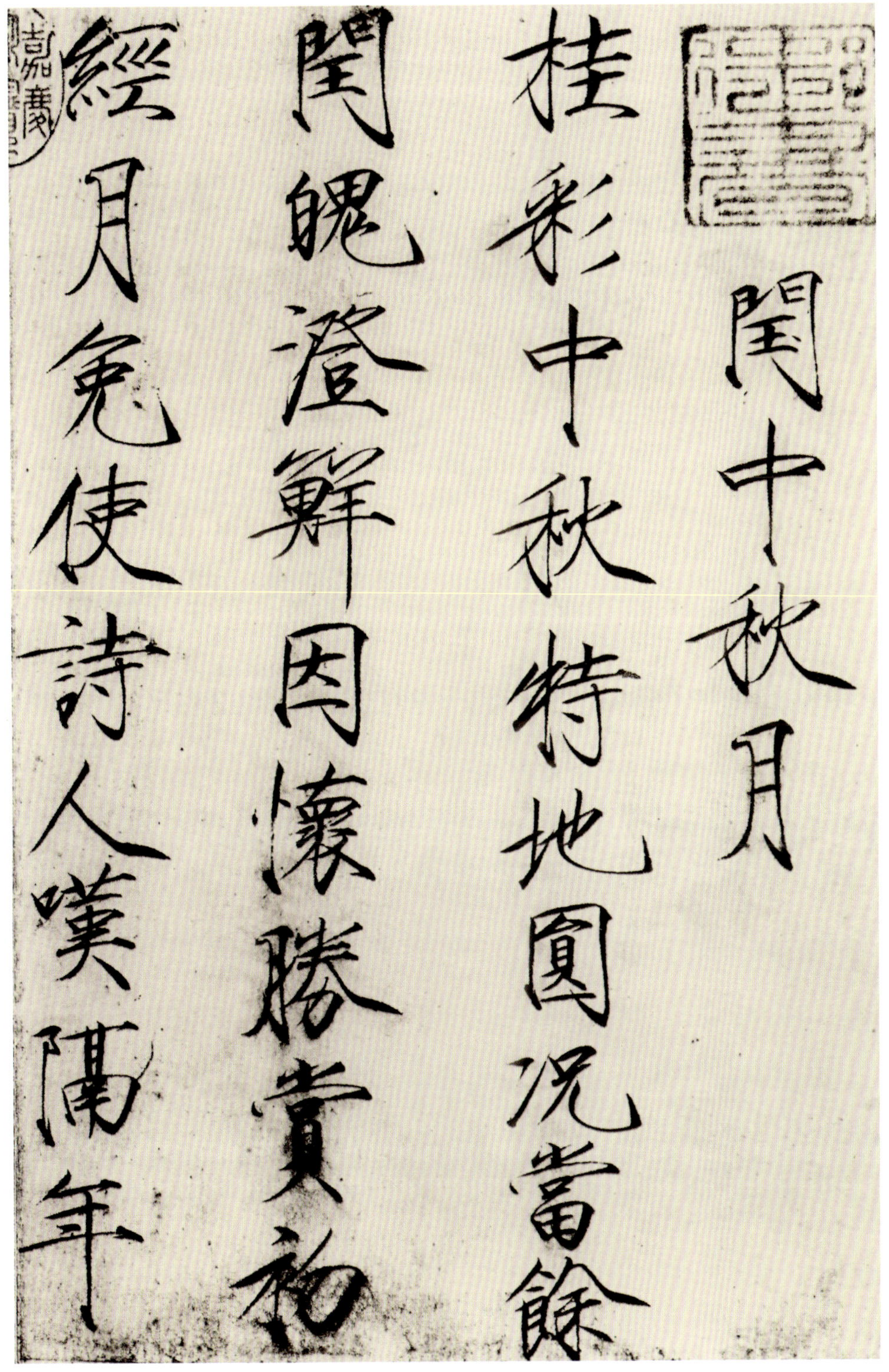

Poem of Moon in the Mid-Autumn Festival (闰中秋月诗, *Run Zhong Qiu Yue Shi*)
Zhao Ji (1082 – 1135, Song Dynasty)
Regular script
35 cm × 44.5 cm
Palace Museum, Beijing

Zhao Ji was notorious for his stupidity and timidity as an emperor of the Song Dynasty. However, he was extremely versed in art, being an expert at flower-bird and figure paintings and calligraphy. He was the founder of the Slender Gold Style of Calligraphy [gold (金, *jin*) here is homophonic to sinew (筋, *jin*) in the Chinese language], which features strokes that are thin and slender, tall and straight, and that unfold themselves naturally, bringing to mind the simple elegance of a book. This work is a typical work of the Slender Gold Style of Calligraphy.

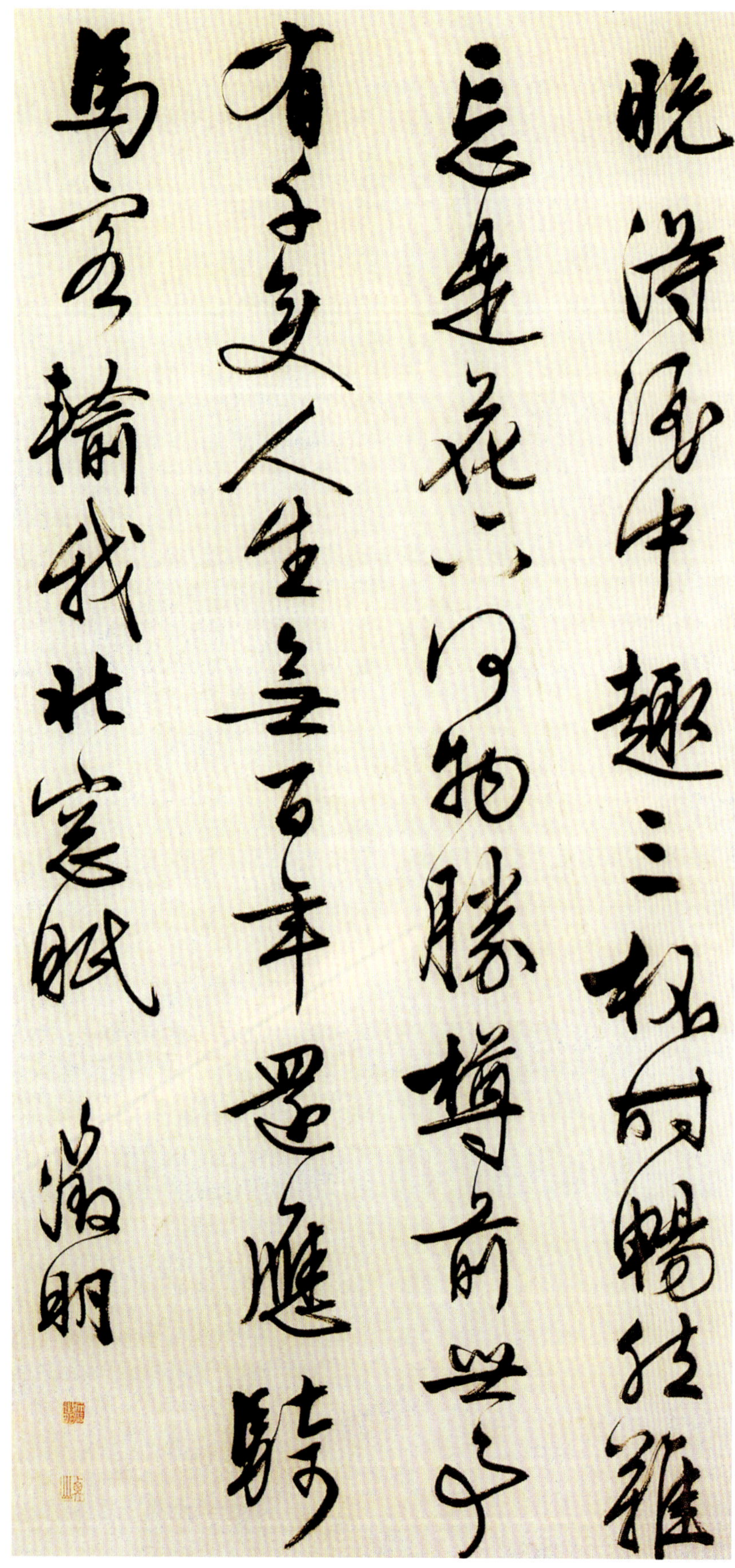

Eight-Line Poem in Five-Character Meter on a Scroll (五律词轴, *Wu Lü Ci Zhou*)
Wen Zhengming (1470 – 1559, Ming Dynasty)
Semi-cursive script
131.5 cm × 63.5 cm
Palace Museum, Beijing

This is a representative work of Wen Zhengming, a well-known calligrapher in the Ming Dynasty. It is simple and meticulous in composition, but vivid and varied in writing style. As a representative work of the calligrapher in his later years, it displays his matured and tactful calligraphic style to the fullest.

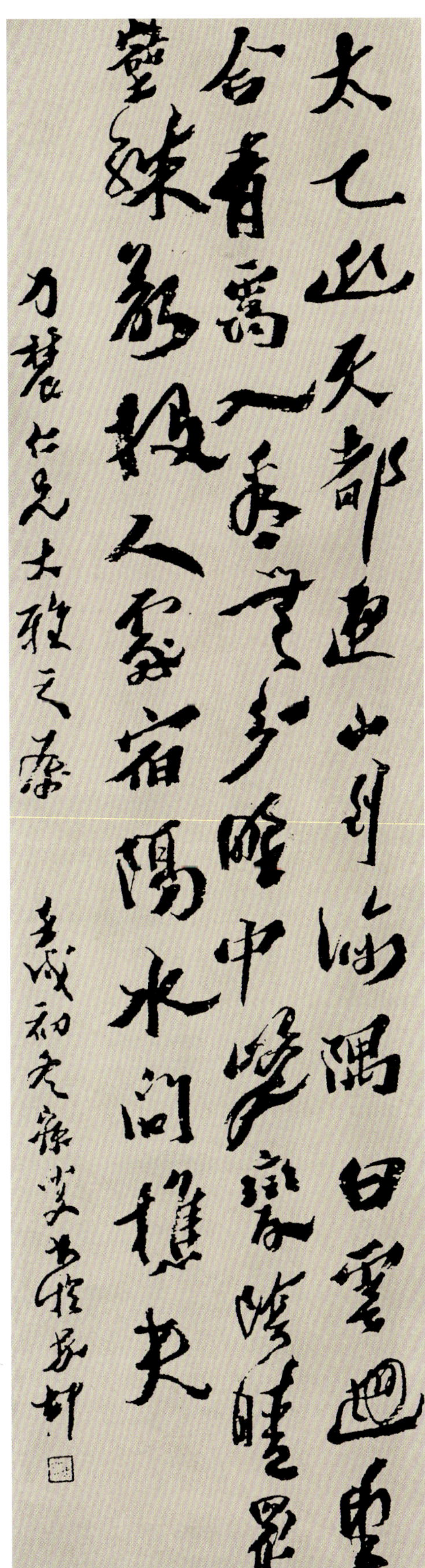

Mount Zhongnan (终南山诗, *Zhong Nan Shan Shi*)
Shen Zengzhi (1850 – 1922)
Semi-cursive script

Shen Zengzhi, who studied model letters before turning to the stele inscriptions, was eventually able to blend the two traditions to create a distinctly personal style. His contemporary Zeng Xi said about his calligraphic style that "his skill shows through an apparent clumsiness; his ingenuity is reflected in his less than fluent brushwork; and his strength lies in instability." The clumsiness and the lack of fluidity come from the brush-tip being moved against the grain of the paper; and the instability results from his giving up the balance in individual characters to seek coordination and balance between characters and columns.

5. A Natural and Flowing Writing Style—Zhao Mengfu and His Semi-Cursive Script

Zhao Mengfu was another artist of supreme versatility after Su Shi. He was well versed in essays, calligraphy, and painting and his running-regular script was known as the "Zhao-style calligraphy." A man of profound learning, Zhao brimmed with talent, was highly proficient in poetry, music, calligraphy, painting, seal cutting, and Buddhism. What's more, he also made brilliant achievements in his official career. His tremendous influence was not confined to the Yuan Dynasty in which he lived, but has lasted until today (Figure 11).

The mid 13th and early 14th century was a turbulent period of dynastic changes in China. The Southern Song Dynasty had just collapsed and the Yuan Dynasty had begun to rule China. Living in such a historical period, Zhao Mengfu had a splendid life filled with ups and downs.

Zhao Mengfu was born in Wuxing, Zhejiang province on September 10, 1254. He was an 11th generation grandson of Zhao Kuangyin (927 – 976), founder of the Song Dynasty, and his great grandfather, grandfather, and father were all high-ranking officials at court. He started to learn calligraphy when he was only five and wrote *One Thousand Character Primer* (千字文, *Qian Zi Wen*). He made unceasing efforts to improve himself at the age of 12 when his father died and his mother, Mrs. Qiu, urged him to be self-reliant and hard-working. He made a leap in his calligraphic skill in 1284 after acquiring three volumes of *Model Letters from the Chunhua Pavilion* (淳化阁帖, *Chun Hua Ge Tie*), a well-known calligraphic work collection of that time. In 1286, at the age of 33, he was recommended by the imperial envoy to pay an audience with Kublai Khan at the Yuan capital of Dadu (Beijing today) and secured an official position. Three years later, he married Guan Daosheng, a decedent of Guan Zhong, a famous prime minister in the Warring States Period (475 – 221 BC). Guan was also an accomplished poet, painter, and calligrapher who, as the author of *Ink Bamboo Painting* (墨竹谱, *Mo Zhu Pu*), was particularly talented in painting ink bamboo with delicate and elegant strokes. This husband and wife team remained devoted to each other to their ripe old age. Zhao Mengfu's son, Zhao Yong (1289 – 1360 BC), was also a master hand in calligraphy, particularly in semi-cursive script. At 42, Zhao Mengfu resigned office and went back to his hometown of Wuxing. However, he was assigned an important position in office at the age of 58 in 1311 after Emperor Renzong ascended to the throne. This time, a title was also conferred upon his whole family, which elevated his social status and influence to another level. His wife died in 1319, which dealt the calligrapher a heavy blow. He stayed in his hometown, seeking guidance from Buddhism and composing a large quantity of calligraphic works. Zhao Mengfu passed away peacefully at home on June 16, 1322. On that very morning, he was still reading and writing and engaging in spirited talks. He was buried alongside his wife in Deqing county, Zhejiang province, China.

Three important factors have contributed

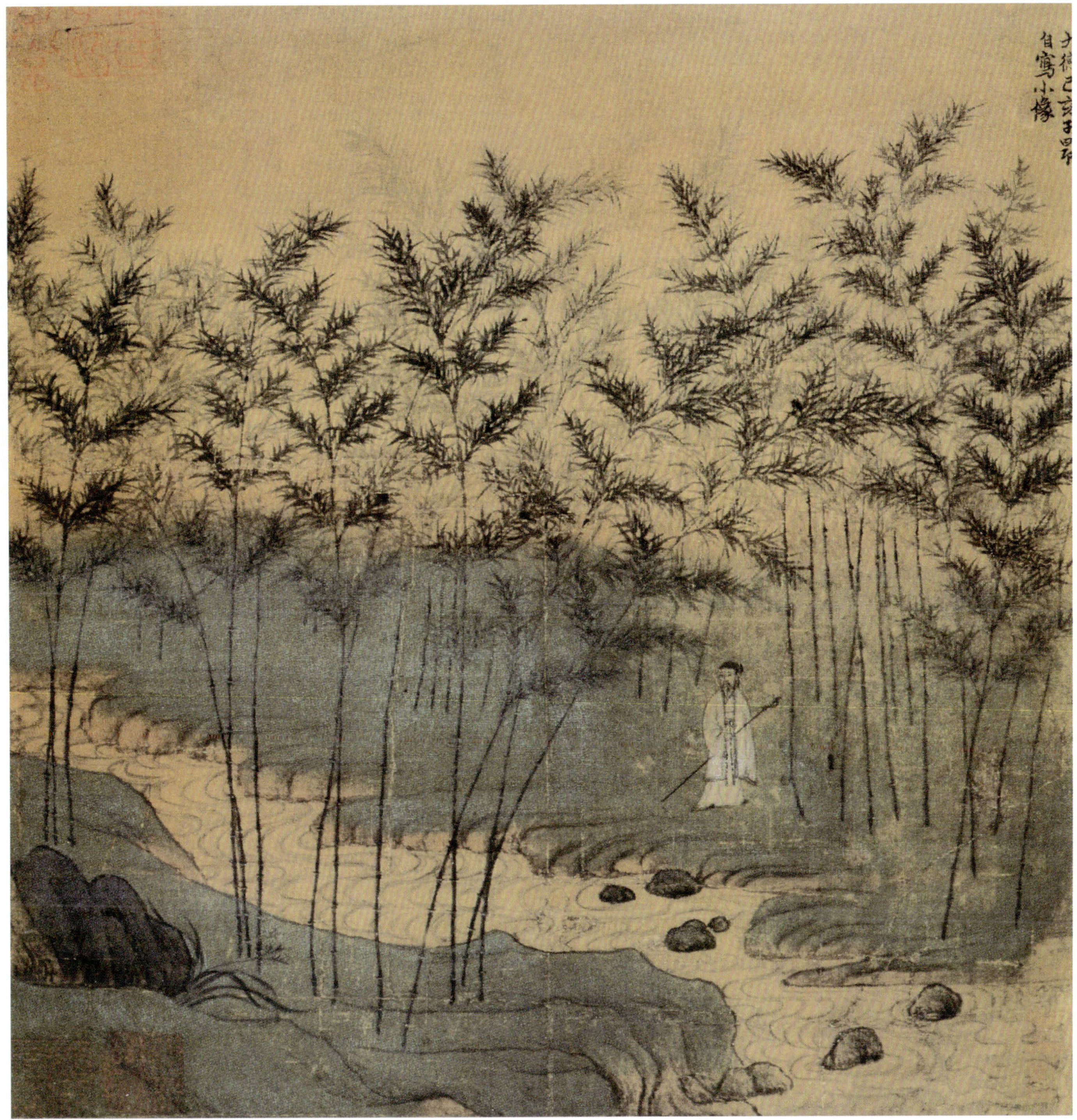

Figure 11
A man brimmed with talent, Zhao Mengfu not only was highly proficient in poetry, music, calligraphy, painting, seal cutting, and Buddhism, but also made brilliant achievements in his official career.

to the success of Zhao Mengfu: the profound influence of his family, the great efforts he spent on practice, and the nurturing of the then natural and humanistic environment, including the art, religious, political, and cultural activities he attended and other calligraphers he befriended.

All the nine emperors and other members of the royal family in the Song Dynasty were lovers of art and literature, among whom there was no lack of highly accomplished artists, the most famous ones being Emperor Huizong, Zhao Ji and Emperor Gaozong, Zhao Gou (1107 – 1185). When Zhao Ji held the throne, he organized scholar-officials to compile *Book on the Art of Calligraphy* (宣和书谱, *Xuan He Shu Pu*) and *Book on the Art of Painting* (宣和画谱, *Xuan He Hua Pu*), both of which are well-known in the Chinese history of art. In addition, he himself was a highly-gifted painter and calligrapher. His regular script was known as Slender Gold Style of Calligraphy, a name that came from the fact that the calligrapher's writing resembles gold filament, twisted and turned. An original and distinctive calligraphic style, this style occupied a very important position in calligraphic history.

Emperor Gaozong established the capital in Lin'an (Hangzhou today). He showed no interest in managing state affairs, but loved calligraphy, cursive script in particular, with great passion. He followed the styles of Wang Xizhi and Wang Xianzhi and wrote precisely and gracefully. A descendant of the royal family, it was inevitable that Zhao Mengfu was influenced by his ancestors. He once wrote several essays showing his respect

One Thousand Character Primer

According to *History of the Liang Dynasty* (梁史, *Liang Shi*), Emperor Wu of Liang ordered Yin Tieshi, a high-ranking official, to find one thousand characters that did not repeat themselves from among the stone inscriptions written by Wang Xizhi, for his sons to learn calligraphy. As single characters devoid of meaning were difficult to remember, he asked the assistant minister Zhou Xingsi to make the characters into a meaningful and readable piece of article.

Going back home, Zhou racked his brain for a whole night and finally came out with the present primer, a long poem with four characters to each line. Consisting of characters that do not repeat each other, the primer is coherent in meaning from beginning to end and beautiful in rhyme and rhythm, containing knowledge about various aspects of life, such as astronomy, nature, moral character cultivation, ethics, geography, history, agriculture, sacrifice, gardening, and daily eating, drinking, and living.

Written in an instructive and interesting manner, it is most ideal for imparting rudimentary knowledge to children, and has since become a classical textbook for children in China across centuries. Meanwhile, calligraphers of different schools in different dynasties have taken the primer as an important text for creation, giving birth to works of different calligraphic styles, the most famous of which is *One Thousand Character Primer in Regular and Cursive Scripts* written by Zhi Yong of the Sui Dynasty.

for them and even deliberately imitated the style of Emperor Gaozong in his early works.

Talented as he was, Zhao Mengfu was still the epitome of diligence, leaving a surprisingly huge number of calligraphic works to later generations. For all his life, he had been absorbing the calligraphy essence of others and had copied no less than several hundred times such famous calligraphic works as *Preface to the Orchid Pavilion Collection* and *Essay on Yue Yi* (乐毅论, *Yue Yi Lun*) by Wang Xizhi, *Ode to the Goddess of Luo River* (洛神赋, *Luo Shen Fu*) by Wang Xianzhi, and *One Thousand Character Primer in Regular and Cursive Scripts* (真草千字文, *Zhen Cao Qian Zi Wen*) by Zhi Yong (510 – 610). He did not slacken his effort to work even when he was over sixty-five years old and in poor health and produced a large number of calligraphic works and paintings. Just as a critic had accurately observed, "Calligraphy is an art of arduous efforts. One may depend either on his talent or his hard work for proficiency. However, if he is both talented and hardworking, he can then achieve a higher level of proficiency in this art, just as Zhao Mengfu has done."

Zhao Mengfu also befriended a lot of other calligraphers; among them were eminent monks, venerable seniors, and talented young artists. They learned from each other and made up for each other's deficiencies. Quite a few existing works of Zhao Mengfu were letters to and from his friends or were written at the invitation of his friends. *First and Second Odes to Red Cliffs* is such a work.

Model Letters from the Chunhua Pavilion

In 992, the 3rd year of Chunhua in the Song Dynasty, Emperor Zhao Jiong, out of his personal love of calligraphy, requested Wang Zhu, a renowned scholar, to sort out the calligraphic works of all ages in the imperial storehouse, get them labeled, and have them carved on jujube wood. It was against this background that *Model Letters from the Chunhua Pavilion* was born and named.

Model Letters from the Chunhua Pavilion is the earliest calligraphic collection in China, embodying 420 calligraphic works of 103 authors, including emperors, ministers, and famous calligraphers, spanning a thousand years and more from the pre-Qin days to the Sui and Tang dynasties.

The collection, reputed to be the "forefather of calligraphic works," comprises a total of ten volumes. The first volume contains the calligraphic works of emperors and rulers in different dynasties, the second, third, and fourth volumes contain the works of famous ministers, the fifth volume contains ancient models of calligraphy for practice, the sixth, seventh, and eighth volumes contain the handwritings of Wang Xizhi, and the ninth and tenth volumes contain the works of Wang Xianzhi.

Ever since its birth, the collection had been engraved for circulation nationwide, producing a far-reaching impact on calligraphy in later generations. Later, a fire in the imperial palace destroyed the original carving of the collection, rendering the early rubbing editions extremely valuable and a treasure of the nation.

6. *First and Second Odes to Red Cliffs* and Its Artistic Features

The two original texts against which the calligraphic work *First and Second Odes to Red Cliffs* was written were both named *Ode to Red Cliffs*, but known among later generations as *First Ode to Red Cliffs* and *Second Ode to Red Cliffs* respectively, for they were completed one after another in different times. The two odes are the representative works of Su Shi. Also referred to as Su Dongpo and a native of Sichuan province, Su Shi was the most prominent writer in the Northern Song Dynasty. He brimmed with talent and had attained remarkable achievements in poetry, *ci* poem, and prose.

However, his life was full of ups and downs. In 1079, he was exiled to the remote frontier Huangzhou (Huanggang county today) in Hubei province to serve an insignificant post, due to his offense of the reformist faction at court. There, he often mixed with the locals, chatting with them over wine to learn about the natural sceneries, local conditions and customs, and more importantly, to find an outlet for his sense of loss and melancholy. Astonishingly, this period also marked the height of Su Shi's artistic creation, as all his masterpieces of calligraphy, poetry and *ci* poem, and prose were composed in this period, including the calligraphic work *Poem to Express Melancholy after Demotion*, the *ci* poem *Remembering Red Cliffs, to the Tune of Nian Nu Jiao* (念奴娇·赤壁怀古, *Nian Nu Jiao Chi Bi Huai Gu*), and the prose *First and Second Odes to Red Cliffs*. The latter two share a similar theme, i.e. narrating the story of the Three Kingdoms (220 – 280) in a revisit to the Red Cliffs and giving vent to his own feelings. Interestingly, the Red Cliffs Su Shi visited is not actually the real place where the battle was waged. However, Chinese readers seem to be more familiar with the Red Cliffs under his pen.

First and Second Odes to Red Cliffs consists of two independent essays, the first completed in the fall of 1082, and the second three months later in the early winter. The essays depicted vividly the author's two visits of the Red Cliffs with his friends. Under his pen, the Red Cliffs were so steep that the moon seemed so far away, so rugged that stones were revealed as water ebbed, and so serene that the water surface was not at all ruffled by the light breeze. In the essays, Su Shi conversed with his friends about the spectacular historical story without inhibition and sighed about the law of "change" and "non-change" in nature, revealing to readers his broad-minded and carefree outlook. However, careful readers might also feel that beneath the unconventionally graceful language is hidden a strong sense of sorrow and melancholy derived from the setbacks in his political pursuits. The lonely crane imbued with a magical flavor that appears at the end of *Second Ode to Red Cliffs* and the dream that can hardly be explained all serve to heighten this feeling. In the two essays, each of which contains less than 900 characters, the author has given full play to his superb language skills, integrating scene description, character depiction, expression of feelings, and argumentation into a whole and presenting what is the realistic and the imaginary interchangeably. Ingenious in diction, profound in meaning, and catchy in rhyme, the essays were not only the masterpieces of Su Shi, but also classics in Chinese prose.

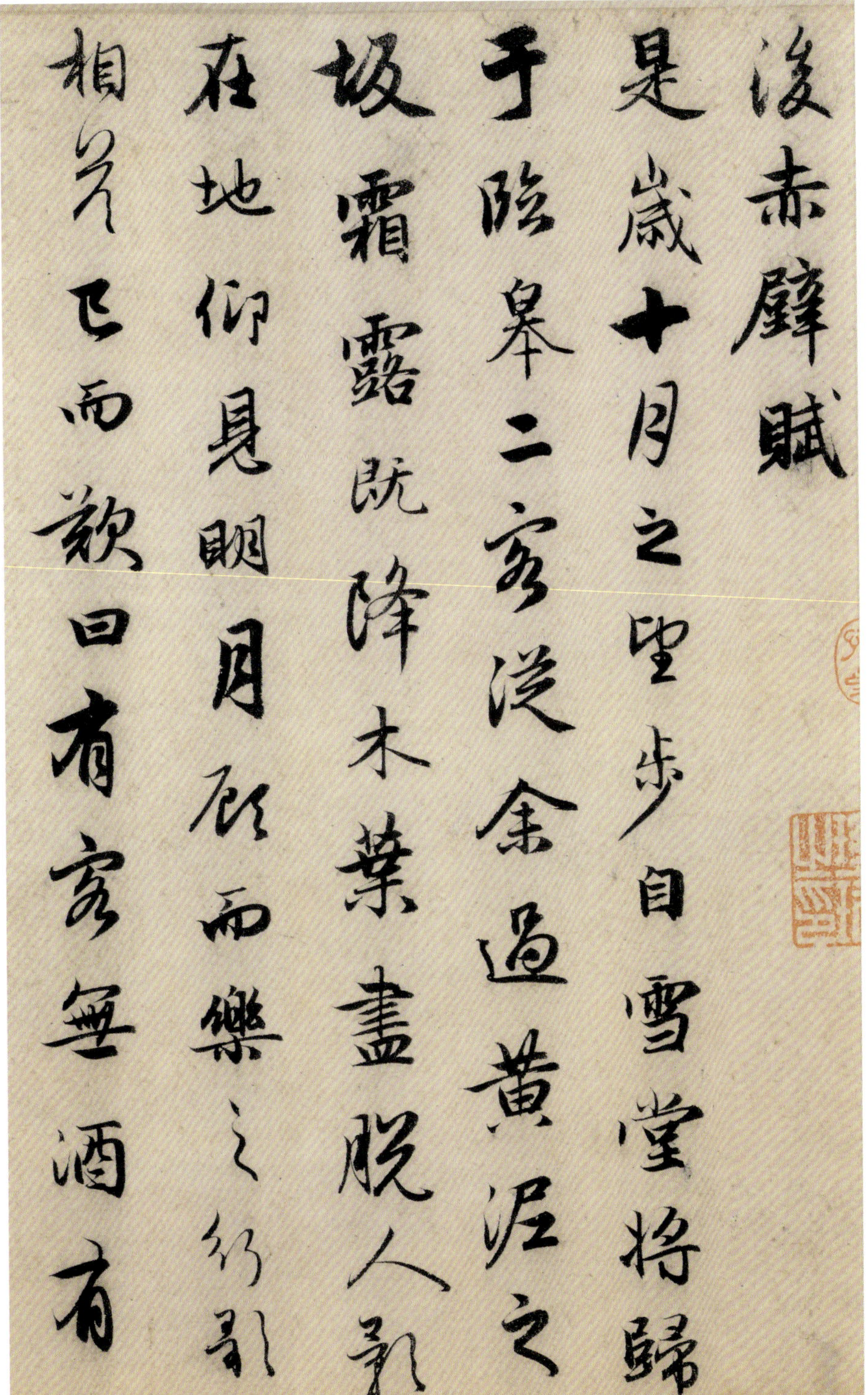

Figure 12
First and Second Odes to Red Cliffs
(前后赤壁赋, *Qian Hou Chi Bi Fu*)
Zhao Mengfu (1254 – 1322)
27.2 cm × 11.1 cm
Palace Museum, Taipei

In terms of visual effect, *First and Second Odes to Red Cliffs* is a perfect representation of the artistic style of *Preface to the Orchid Pavilion Collection*. The overall layout is open and bright, the writing speed is moderate, each of the characters is elegant and beautiful, and the writing technique is smooth and fluent.

One of the peculiar features of *Preface to the Orchid Pavilion Collection* lies in the Chinese character 之, which assumes different postures in different places under the pen of Wang Xizhi. Likewise, 之 in this work also presents varied shapes and postures. In addition, some characters that have appeared repeatedly in this work, such as 水 (water, *shui*), 月 (moon, *yue*), 天 (heaven, *tian*), and 地 (earth, *di*), are also treated differently in different places, either prostrating or looking up or extending themselves freely. Instead of sedulously imitating Wang Xizhi's writing techniques, Zhao Mengfu in his own works has attained fidelity to Wang's calligraphy both in form and spirit, reproducing the latter's moderate and steady style with ease. *First and Second Odes to Red Cliffs* is exactly such a work.

Two hundred years later in the Yuan Dynasty, Zhao Mengfu, an erudite scholar who admired Su Shi, emerged as the most renowned calligrapher of that time. One day, at the invitation of his friend, he readily wrote *First and Second Odes to Red Cliffs* in semi-cursive script on the top-grade paper his friend brought (Figure 12). To show his respect for Su Shi, he painted a portrait of the poet on the top of his calligraphy. In the picture, Su Shi is properly dressed, holding a bamboo stick in his hand and looking happy and unperturbed, a true literary giant in every sense of the word. With flowing lines and a balanced use of ink, the picture is a masterpiece of Zhao Mengfu's water-ink figure paintings (Figure 13).

This work, completed in 1301, contains 935

Battle of Red Cliffs

In 208, the 13th year of Jian'an in the Han Dynasty, Cao Cao, the northern warlord, planned to conquer the land south of the Yangtze River, after his successful reunification of the north. In October, he marched his troops eastward personally, ready to battle it out with the southern warlords Liu Bei and Sun Quan. Zhuge Liang, an accomplished military strategist serving Liu Bei, encouraged Liu to combine forces with Sun Quan in a fight against Cao Cao. After much persuasion and meticulous analysis, he finally convinced Sun Quan to agree to the alliance. By then, the military forces between the two sides were in sharp contrast: the southern side had eighty thousand men, while the northern side had two hundred thousand.

Afterwards, Zhou Yu, who was a powerful general of Sun Quan, joined forces with Liu Bei, and the allied forces sailed upstream to the Red Cliffs (Chibi in Hubei province today) and encountered Cao Cao's vanguard force there in a skirmish. By then, Cao Cao had moored his ships from stem to stern, aiming to reduce seasickness in his navy, which comprised mostly northerners who were not used to living on ships. He drilled his navy day and night, awaiting a chance for a decisive engagement. Zhou Yu, on the other hand, moored his warships at the Red Cliffs, confronting his opponent across the Yangtze River.

On the day of the battle, Huang Gai, a divisional commander of Zhou Yu, sent Cao Cao a letter feigning surrender and prepared a squadron of capital ships. The ships had been converted into fire ships by filling them with bundles of kindling, dry reeds, and fatty oil. As Huang Gai's "defecting" squadron approached the midpoint of the river, the sailors applied fire to the ships before taking to small boats. The unmanned fire ships, carried by the southeastern wind, sped towards Cao Cao's fleet and set it ablaze. Within a short time, smoke and flames stretched across the sky, and a large number of men and horses either burned to death or drowned. Following the initial shock, Zhou Yu and the allies led a lightly armed force to capitalize on the assault. The northern army was thrown into confusion and was utterly defeated, and Cao Cao was forced to retreat to Jiangling.

The Battle of Red Cliffs was a large-scale river battle that was waged for the first time in the Yangtze River Valley in Chinese history. It is a classical example of the few defeating the many on the battlefield, rendering it impossible for Cao Cao to reunite the country in a short time and determining the balance of power between the three kingdoms of Wei, Shu, and Wu.

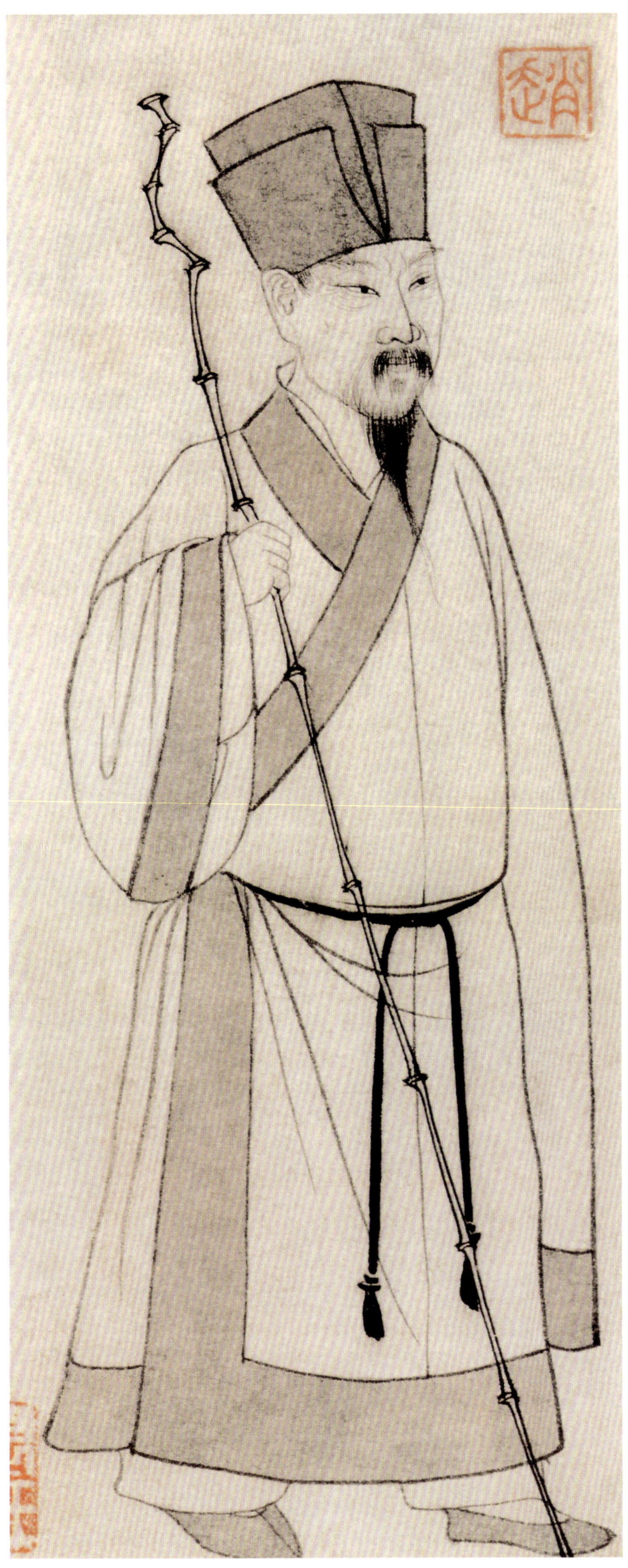

characters in 81 lines. Aside from the texts, there is a paragraph at the bottom written by the calligrapher himself, explaining the time and place the calligraphy was done and the fact that it was done at the invitation of a friend. Judging from this paragraph and the overall effect of this work, Zhao Mengfu might be rather light-hearted at the time of writing and might have finished the work in one go with facility. Though Zhao admired the calligraphy of the Song Dynasty, including those of Su Shi, Huang Tingjian, and Mi Fu, this work, nevertheless, was the result of his persistent learning of the two Wangs, particularly Wang Xizhi. For all his life, he had been painstakingly pursuing and learning the calligraphy of Wang Xizhi and had copied such works as *Preface to the Orchid Pavilion Collection* time and time again. Therefore, he had achieved an extremely refined understanding of almost all the minute aspects of Wang's semi-cursive script, from the dots and strokes, the style, structure, composition of the character, to the tone of his works and the spirit they convey.

Zhao Mengfu was 48 years old when *First and Second Odes to Red Cliffs* was completed. He was then in the heyday of his artistic growth and his semi-cursive script, a style of calligraphy he excelled at, had gradually matured.

Figure 13
Zhao Mengfu painted a portrait of Su Shi on the top of his calligraphy of the *First and Second Odes to Red Cliffs*. With flowing lines and a balanced use of ink, the picture described a true literary giant in every sense of the word.

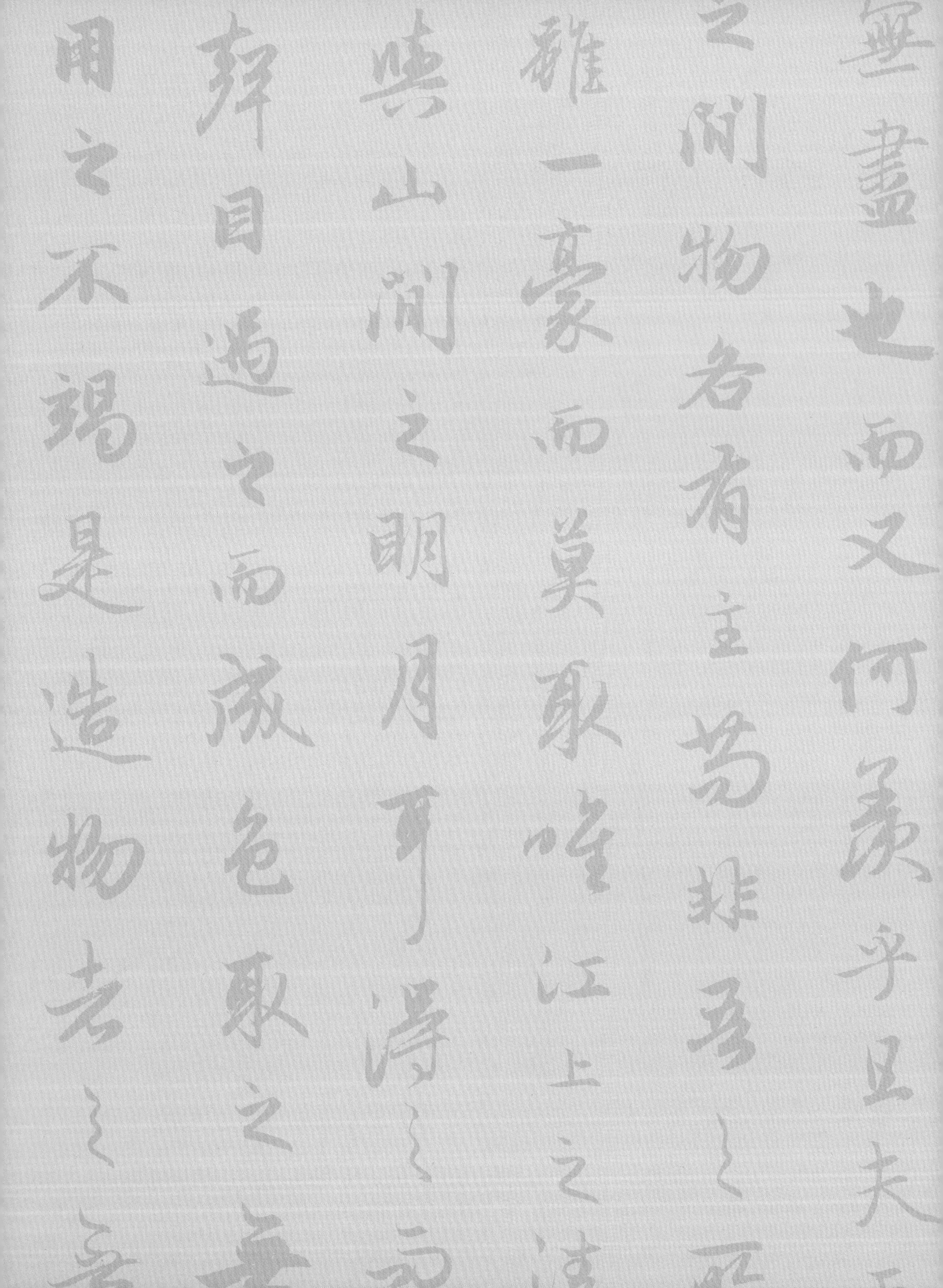
無盡也而又何羨乎且夫
之間物各有主苟非吾之
雖一毫而莫取惟江上之
與山間之明月耳得之而
聲目遇之而成色取之
用之不竭是造物者之

Chapter Two

Writing Preparation

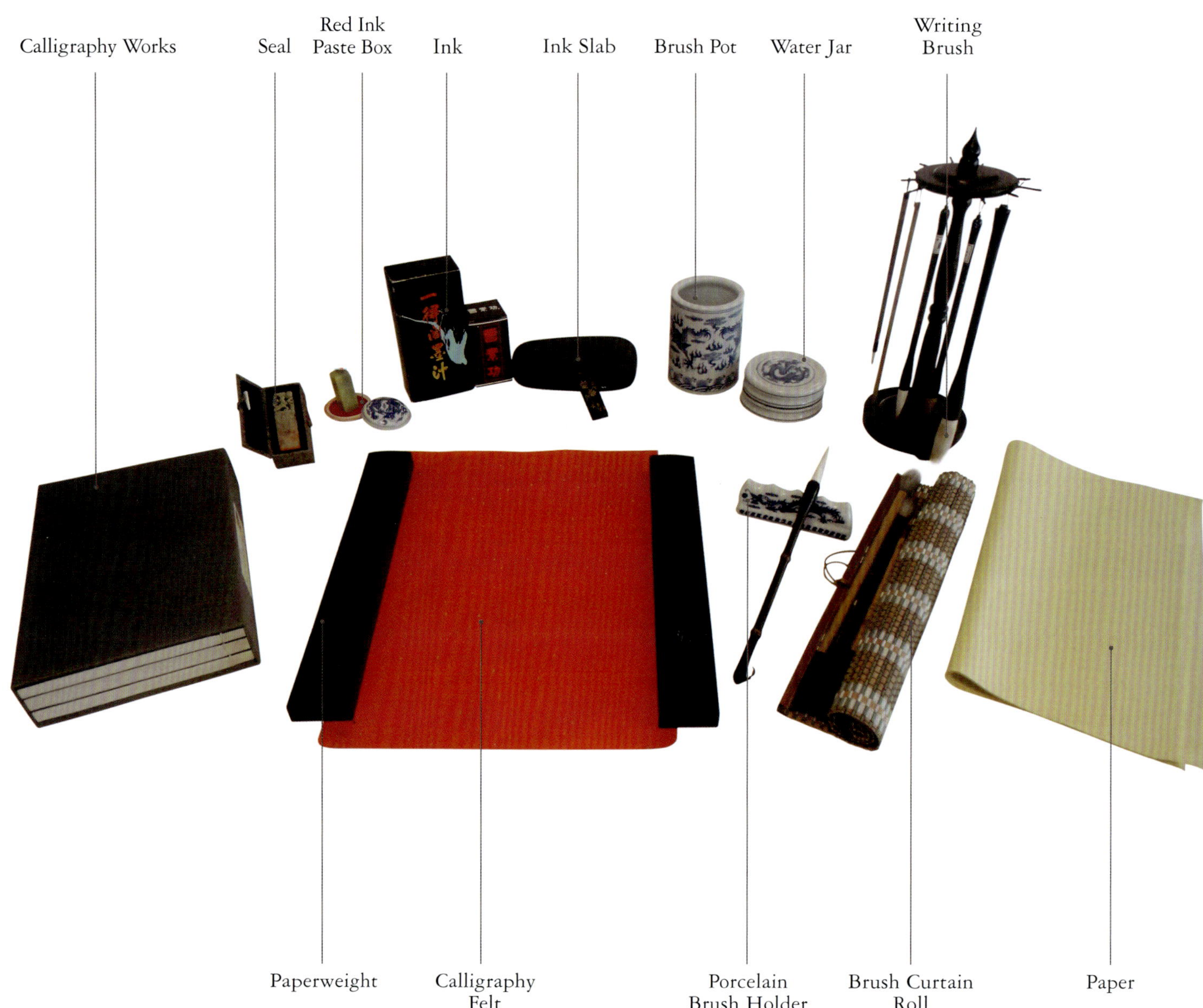

Figure 14
The Treasures of a Chinese Scholar's Study

Calligraphic works are a fine mirror of the emotions and moral standards of calligraphers. And this is especially true of semi-cursive script. Before practicing semi-cursive script, one should first strike a sympathetic chord with the work in question and then maintain a peaceful state of mind. Equally important are the choice of writing tools, the way the writing brush is held, the control over the brush with the wrist and elbow, and the posture of the body.

1. Writing Tools: The Four Treasures of the Study

The writing brush, ink, paper, and ink slab are collectively known as "the four treasures of the study." They are not only the tools of writing and painting, but also essential items in the study of a scholar that show his social status and aesthetic tastes. A good knowledge of their functions, maintenance, selection, and use is essential for any learners of calligraphy (Figure 14).

Writing Brush

A writing brush consists of a shaft and a head which is usually made from the hair of a wide variety of animals and is thus elastic and ink-absorptive. The brush is capable of presenting lines with numerous changes based on the changing mood of the calligrapher, the direction it is wielded, the force of lift and press, and the dryness and moistness of ink. It is the most essential of the "four treasures."

Writing brushes fall into different kinds. In terms of hair texture, there are brushes with soft, hard, and mixed hairs. The soft hair is mainly goat hair that absorbs ink well and is capable of presenting with vigor the calligrapher's rich and diversified use of ink. Writing brushes of this kind are ideal for regular script in big characters, seal script, and clerical script. The hard hair is mainly made from the hairs of wolves, the bristles of wild horses, and the mustache of mice, and thus enjoys fine fluidity of ink. Writing brushes of this kind are the best choice for regular script in small characters and sturdy running-cursive script. The mixed hair consists of at least two kinds of hair and is neither too flexible nor too stiff. Writing brushes of this kind suit beginners of calligraphy. In terms of hair size, there are big, medium, and small brushes. Small brushes are extensive in use and easy to wield. They are the first choice for beginners.

A good writing brush should have an upright and straight shaft and should be comfortable to hold. The hair should be sharply pointed, neatly cut, smoothly round, and highly flexible, able to resume its original shape immediately when pressed.

Before a new brush is used, soak it fully in cold or mild water (but never in hot water). After each use, immediately clean it with cold water, gently squeeze the hair with your hand, wash away the remnant ink, shape the hair into a cone, and hang it up to dry. That way, your brush is clean and ready for the next use.

Ink

In early times, people used natural graphite and mineral pigment as the materials to write with. By the Western Zhou Dynasty (1046 – 771 BC), they had learned to make ink by mixing the soot from the burning of oil and tree branches with animal glue and medicinal ingredients. And the ink that was made fell into three categories: oil soot ink, pine soot ink, and carbon soot ink.

The way to grind ink is worthy of careful study. First, place a little water in the ink slab, and then rub the ink stick with well-distributed strength clockwise until the ink becomes thick. Quality ink is fine-grained, deep-colored, and contains less glue. It feels smooth and produces a slight and thin sound when grinded. As each grind produces ink of different thickness, the several characters or lines of characters the calligrapher finishes in one go with each dip of his brush in the ink usually grow fainter in color and become dryer. Therefore, the lingering charm brought about by the use of ink in a calligraphic work can show the pauses of the calligrapher in the writing process. Last but not least, grind only the ink you need for that day, and do not permit ink to dry in the ink stone.

Prepared Chinese ink was invented in the Qing Dynasty, which could be used directly without being grinded. Due to the fast pace of modern life, most calligraphers today would choose prepared Chinese ink for their artistic creation. However, it is strongly recommended that you use as much ink as you need each time and do not pour the rest of the ink back into the ink bottle in case it goes bad.

Paper

In the Western Han Dynasty, people tried to make paper with hemp. In 105, Cai Lun (61 – 121), a famous inventor, made paper with more practical use by improved technology, providing a fine carrier for China's calligraphic and painting art.

The paper often used by Chinese calligraphers and painters includes rice paper (*xuanzhi*), bamboo paper (*yuanshuzhi*), mulberry paper (*pizhi*), and silk paper (*juan*), the most popular of which is rice paper, which is usually classified into raw rice paper (*shengxuan*), ripe rice paper (*shuxuan*), and half-ripe rice paper (*banshuxuan*) based on different production methods. Raw rice paper, which is not specially processed, excels in its ability to absorb water, causing the ink on it to blur. Ripe rice paper, however, is smeared on by potassium alum during its production, which results in its texture being harder and its ability to absorb water weaker. Half-ripe rice paper has intermediate absorbability, between raw rice paper and ripe rice paper.

The calligrapher selects paper according to his personal likes and the characteristics of the script he is to write. Normally, raw rice paper is ideal for semi-cursive and cursive scripts. It is recommended for beginners who copy *First and Second Odes to Red Cliffs* to use bamboo paper or paper made of bamboo fiber, for they are steady in performance and moderate in price. They may choose half-ripe rice paper for genuine creation of calligraphic works.

Rice paper must be kept away from humidity and oil smoke. It can be placed in the study or at an elevated place in the room and should be dried once or twice a year to rid humidity.

Ink Slab

An ink slab is a mortar for the grinding and containment of ink. It is usually made of stone or mud, but occasionally of pottery and porcelain. In ancient time, light green ink slabs were considered the most precious, then bluish-purple or bluish-black ones, then purple ones, and lastly grayish-black ones, which were regarded as inferior.

For beginners who want to choose an ink slab, he should first feel the surface of the ink slab with his fingers. It needs to be smooth and warm like a baby's skin. It needs to be hard and heavy and can deliver a clear crystalline sound when stricken gently. A fine ink slab remains cold even in midsummer. Second, he can also find a good ink slab by rubbing the same ink stick with the same water and strength on different ink slabs. A fine ink slab needs fewer rubbings to make ink and seems to be passionately attached to the ink in it.

Ink slabs need to be cleaned from time to time with water that is not too hot. In ancient time, people washed the surface of the ink slab with withered lotus seed-pots, but today we can use water and a sponge or any other soft, water-absorbing material for cleaning. Do not soak the ink slab in water for a long time if it is not in use and dry it before it is laid up.

2. Writing Postures

Writing postures here mainly refer to the body and wrist positions of the writer and the way the writing brush is held.

There are two basic body positions for writing Chinese calligraphy: sitting or standing.

In a sitting position, you should sit naturally and steadily, keeping your head, body, arms, and feet well coordinated with each other. The head should be slightly forward and the eyes fixed straight and even on the spot where you intend to write. The body should be erect, the shoulders balanced, the back straight, and the distance between you and the table appropriate. The arms should be slightly apart, the right hand holding the brush, and the left hand gently holding down the paper. The legs should remain separated, the feet even and firm on the ground. This way, all the body parts are in proper places, and then you can concentrate on your right hand which holds the brush and make sure that every character you write down is a success (Figure 15).

Those who often write large characters or who have acquired some basic writing skills use the standing position. It normally falls into three categories: (1) bend the upper part of your body forward and write with your elbow off the table; (2) when writing on the wall or a board hanging as high as yourself, fix your eyes horizontally or look up at the place you intend to write, and write with your arms moving about freely and smoothly; (3) when writing extremely big characters, spread the paper flat out on the floor, bend over, hold the specially made big brush with both hands, and write with great vigor (Figure 16).

In writing semi-cursive script, you often need to use your wrist to give strength to each wielding of the brush, so that the brush tip will keep moving and turning. You should also try to keep

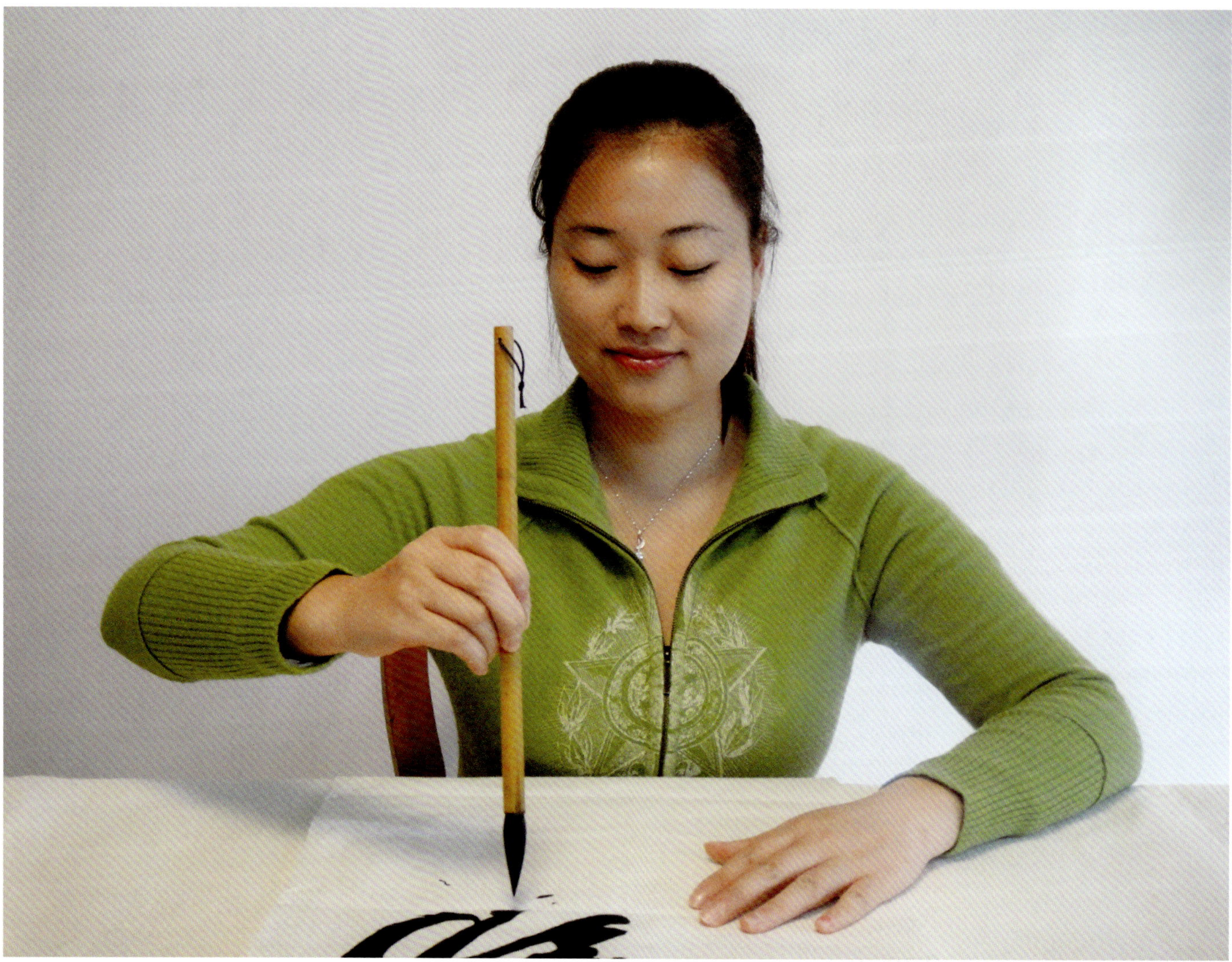

Figure 15
Writing Chinese Calligraphy in Sitting Position

your palm perpendicular and your wrist and elbow horizontal with the paper. Only in this way can the strength of your elbow and arm be passed on to your finger and palm through your wrist and the calligraphy thus written can be more vigorous and powerful. In writing bigger characters, you need to lift your right wrist from the table. Do not feel nervous about your writing posture, as you can adjust it when necessary in the writing process (Figure 17).

The ways to hold the writing brush are many in Chinese calligraphic history. Among them, the "five-finger brush holding method" is the most practiced. Each of the five fingers has its own place and they work together to hold the brush steadily and perform the functions of *an* (按), *ya* (压), *gou* (钩), *ding* (顶), and *di* (抵) in Chinese (Figure 18). The palm does not actually work. It is hollow and shaped like holding an egg. The places the fingers hold vary depending on the script to write. Normally, in writing regular script, you can hold the brush lower so that it is wielded more steadily; in writing running-cursive script, you can hold the brush higher, so that it

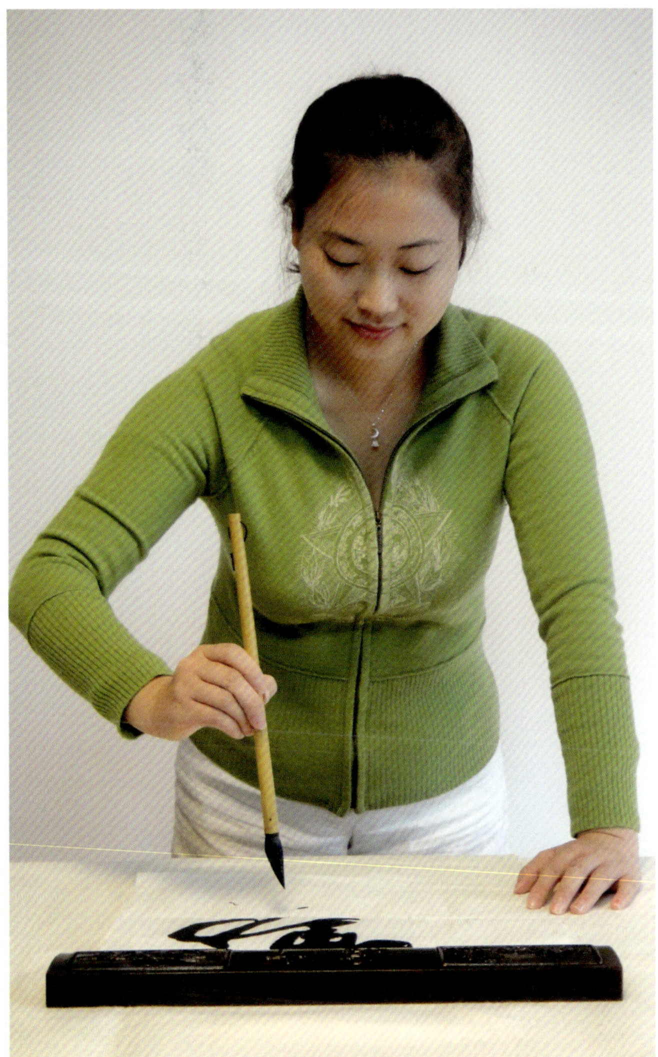

Figure 16
Writing Chinese Calligraphy in Standing Position

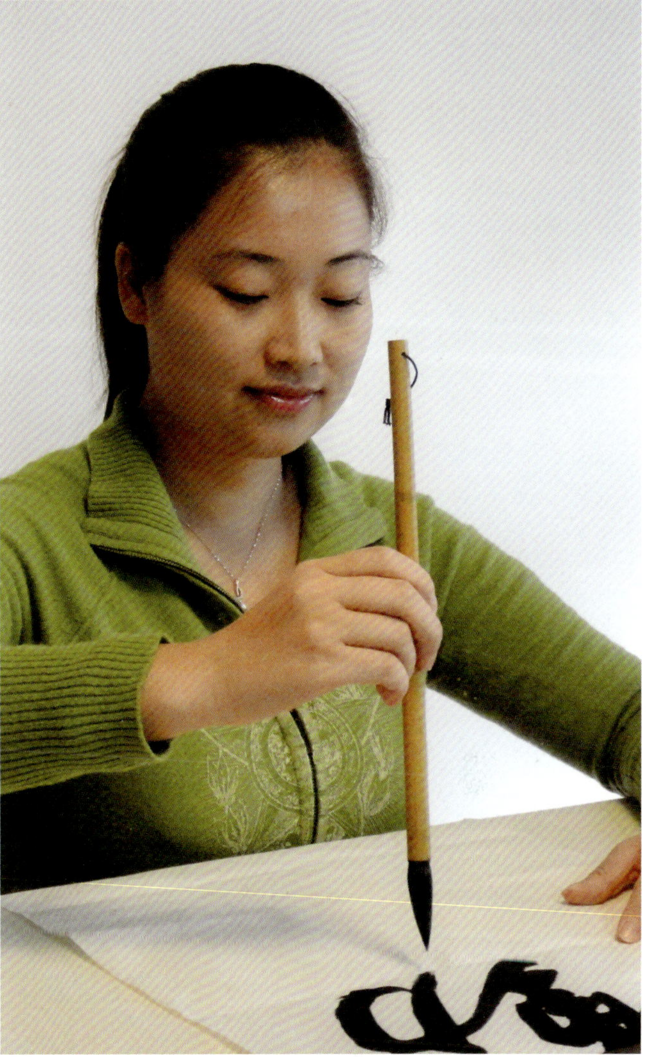

Figure 17
Use your wrist to give strength to each wielding of the brush.

moves quickly and agilely.

Specifically, the five fingers perform the following functions:

An, means that the thumb presses the brush shaft at the first knuckle from inside to outside;

Ya, means that the index finger holds the brush shaft at the first or second knuckle from outside to inside;

Gou, means that the middle finger hooks the brush shaft alongside the index finger;

Ding, means that the ring finger is placed on the inside of the brush shaft at the root of the fingernail pressing the index and middle fingers from the inside to the outside;

Di, refers to the work of the little finger, which is placed under the ring finger to help it.

Aside from the "five-finger brush holding method," the writing brush may also be held with three fingers or four fingers. In general, the way the brush is held varies according to the writer's physiological conditions and personal habits. The brush can also be held with the left hand.

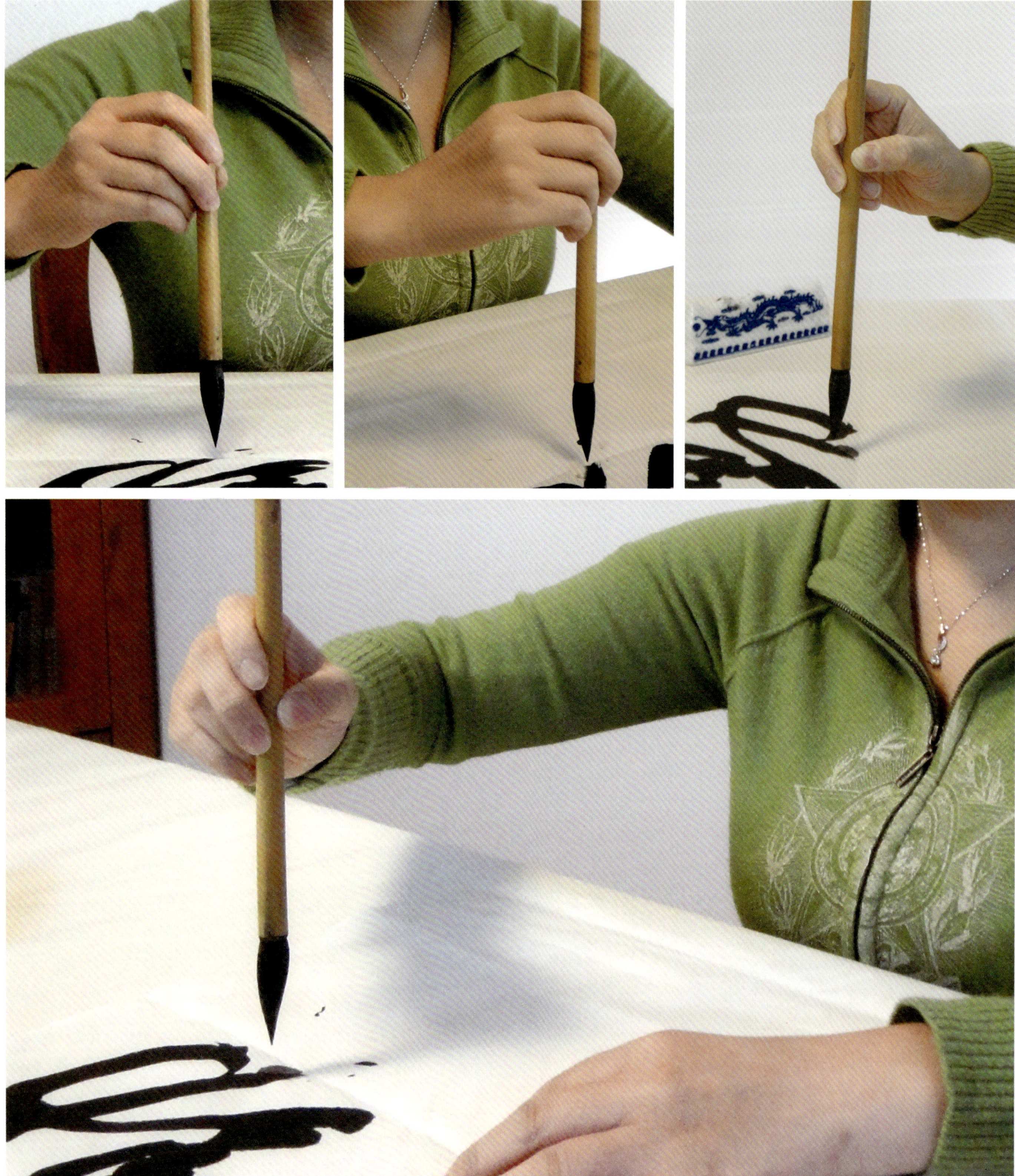

Figure 18
The "five-finger brush holding method" is the most practiced way to hold the writing brush. Each of the five fingers has its own place and they work together to hold the brush steadily.

3. Basic Writing Techniques

Writing techniques refer to the methods of holding and wielding the writing brush. They contribute directly to the diversified changes of lines, light or heavy, quick or slow, diagonal or vertical, crooked or straight. Chinese calligraphy boasts ever-changing strokes and lines, giving readers a strong sense of power and motion.

Lift the brush: This means lifting the brush away from the paper with the fingers holding it via the strength of the arm or wrist. In writing long and thin strokes, you must see to it that each brush lift is concrete and sure, bringing with it a sufficient amount of ink. The strokes written should be thin, round, and solid, rather than light and floating.

Press the brush: This means pressing the brush down with force and making the ink from the brush pour down onto the paper. With a powerful press, the brush, like an awl being nailed down into the ground, assumes a force that seems to be able to penetrate through the paper. Sometimes, to make a second press, you may lift the brush slightly while pressing it down. This way, the brush alternates between lifting up and pressing down, producing stokes that are heavy and more solid.

Begin the stroke: Normally, there are two ways to begin the stroke: *cangfeng* and *loufeng*. *Cangfeng* means hiding the tip of the brush in order to contain one's energy or vitality. It is usually realized by turning the tip in the direction opposite the one intended. For example, if you want to write a stroke from left to right, begin it by pressing the brush tip to the right and then moving your brush a bit to the left to write the stroke to the right. Similarly, if you want to write a stroke from top to bottom, begin it by pressing the brush tip to the bottom and then moving your brush a bit to the top to write the stroke to the bottom. *Loufeng* is in fact a variation of *cangfeng*, which means a deliberate revelation of the cutting power of your brush. The *loufeng* method of wielding your brush means that the tip of the brush goes directly in the direction intended, instead of from the opposite direction. *Loufeng* is particularly common in Zhao Mengfu's calligraphic works.

Wield the brush: *Zhongfeng* and *cefeng* are the most often used techniques of wielding the brush. *Zhongfeng*, or the central cutting power of the brush, means always keeping your brush tip in the middle of the stroke and *cefeng* means using the brush point in a sidelong manner. In the calligraphic works of Zhao Mengfu, most of the strokes are started with sidelong brush tips, which are then moved to the middle of the strokes, producing strokes that look mellow and full. In addition, such moves are also frequently visible in writing bend and hook strokes. Put it figuratively, the inter-conversion between *zhongfeng* and *cefeng* can be compared to someone who rides a bicycle. He must ride in a zigzag direction to maintain balance.

End the stroke: The two normal ways to end your stroke are *huifeng* and *loufeng*. *Huifeng* means the hook-like movement towards the reverse direction at the end of the stroke. It enables the brush tip to bounce back to the upright position. *Loufeng,* as mentioned above, means the tip of the brush does not come from the opposite direction. You do not keep the cutting power of the brush within the stroke, but reveal it outwardly. Most of the strokes in regular script, except the left-falling, right-falling, and straight vertical strokes, are ended with a hook-like movement. In semi-cursive script, the last stroke of a character, which is often directly followed by another stroke that starts the next character, often goes in the direction intended.

4. Basic Strokes of Chinese Characters: Eight Principles of the Character *Yong*

The Eight Principles of the Character *Yong* explain how to write the eight common strokes which are all found in the one character 永 (meaning forever or permanence). They are believed to be the basic strokes of Chinese calligraphy, from which other strokes are derived. The eight strokes are not isolated; instead, they work in combination to mirror the endless charm of Chinese characters.

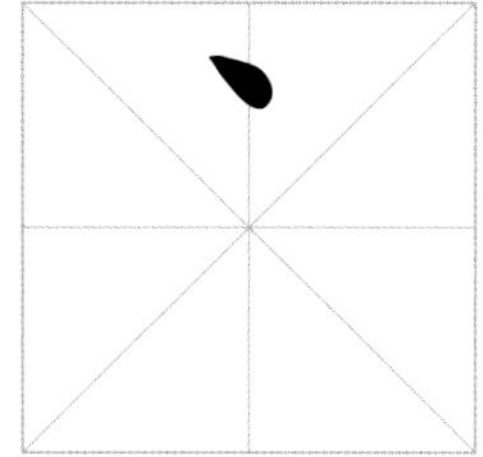

Dot: The dot was known in ancient time as *ce* (侧), which means slanted or not upright. It looks like a huge, magnificently positioned stone standing inclined to one side, precipitous and sturdy. The dot is not only an independent stroke, but also one that begins or ends other strokes. As Chinese calligraphy emphasizes the accumulation of dots into lines, it is particularly important to learn the techniques of writing dots.

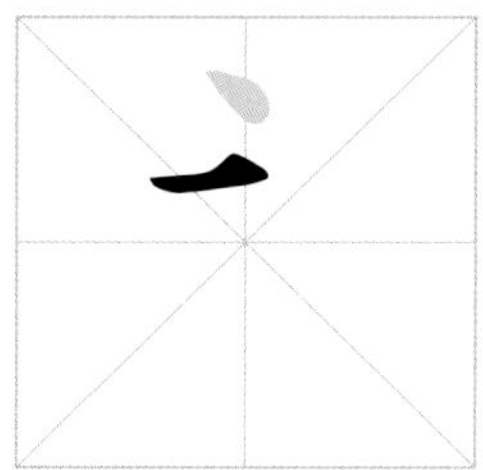

Horizontal: The horizontal was known in ancient time as *le* (勒), which means reigning in a horse. The way to write the horizontal is like a rider reigning in a horse, displaying the momentum of an upward tilt.

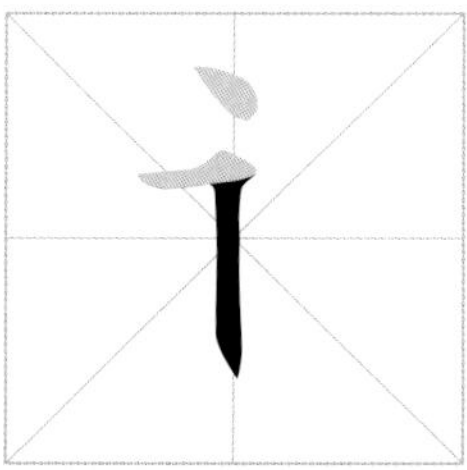

Perpendicular: The perpendicular was known in ancient time as *nu* (弩), which means crossbow. It is a downward stroke showing the momentum of marching forward.

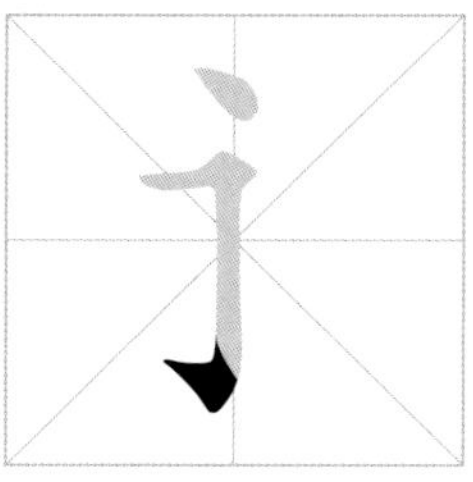

Hook: The hook was known in ancient time as *ti* (趯), which means jumping. In writing the hook, you must first make a hook-like movement with your brush towards the reverse direction, and then, after the brush tip is resumed to an upright position, concentrate your strength on the brush tip before you make a fast tick outwards. Remember, the brush needs to reach the very end of the tick. Writing a hook is like making a jump. First, you need to crouch down to garner strength and then you jump up all of a sudden with dynamism.

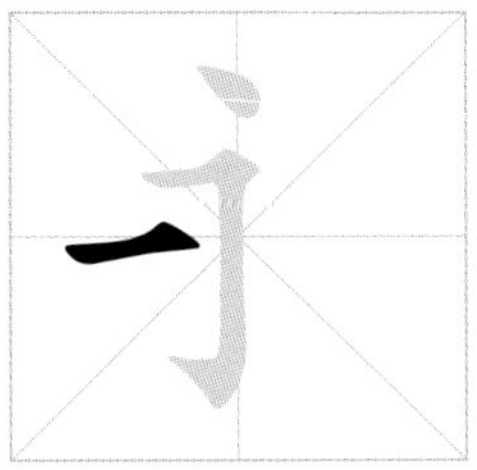

Raise: The raise was known in ancient time as *ce* (策), which means acting in concert. It often appears on the left side of a character and slants upwards toward the right, acting in concert with a stroke on the right side of the character and looking like two people bowing back to back against each other.

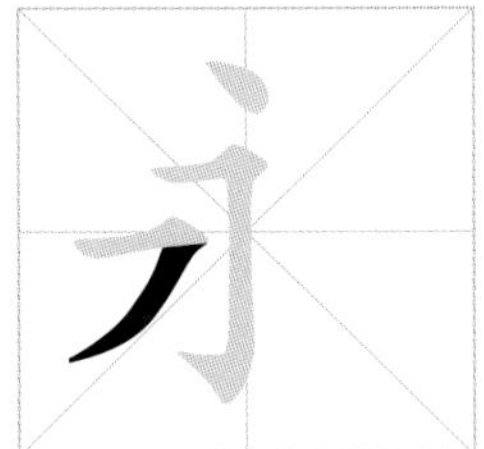

Left-falling stroke: The left-falling stroke was known in ancient time as *lue* (掠), which means sweeping past. The way this stroke is written is like gently brushing the surface of something with your hand. The writing brush is wielded increasingly fast and its tip moves nimbly and briskly. This stroke is noted for its unrestrained grace and agility, but it requires you to deliver your strength right to the end to avoid being shaky and feeble.

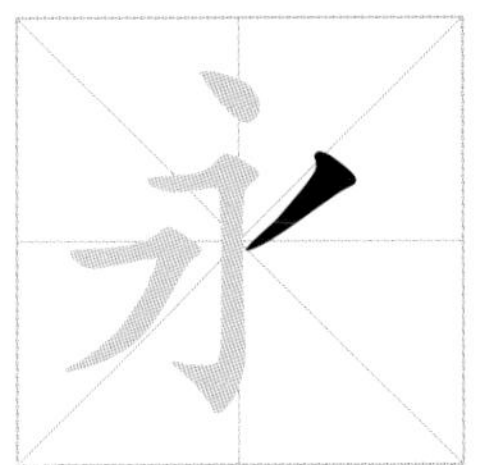

Short slant: The short slant was known in ancient time as *zhuo* (啄), which means pecking. The way the short slant is written resembles birds pecking at their food, fast and agile. The stroke, sharp and acute, falls leftwards with a slight curve. It is noted for its agility and forcefulness.

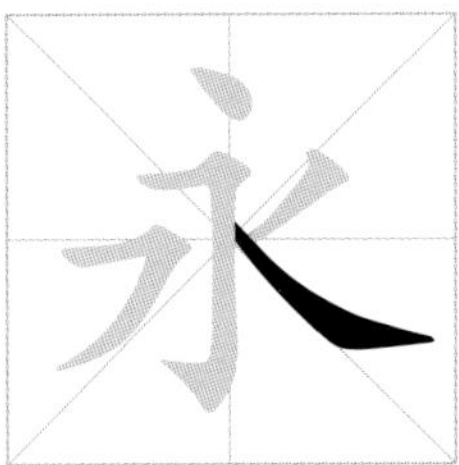

Wave: The wave was known in ancient time as *zhe* (磔), which means dismembering. It has three bends with different momentums and directions, and requires natural and smooth transitions in between. You need to be firm and forceful in writing this stroke.

飛此非曹孟德之詩乎東
西望武昌山川相繆鬱乎
非孟德之困於周郎者乎
荊州下江陵順流而東也
千里旌旗蔽空釃酒臨
槊賦詩固一世之雄也而

Chapter Three

Exercises

1. Basic Strokes

The character strokes in *First and Second Odes to Red Cliffs* are well developed and beautiful, most begin with the brush tip going in the direction intended. The strokes are often interconnected with each other naturally and vividly. The characters are on the side of oblate, unfolding naturally following the momentum of each other. They are graceful in structure and show a flowing beauty.

Long Horizontal

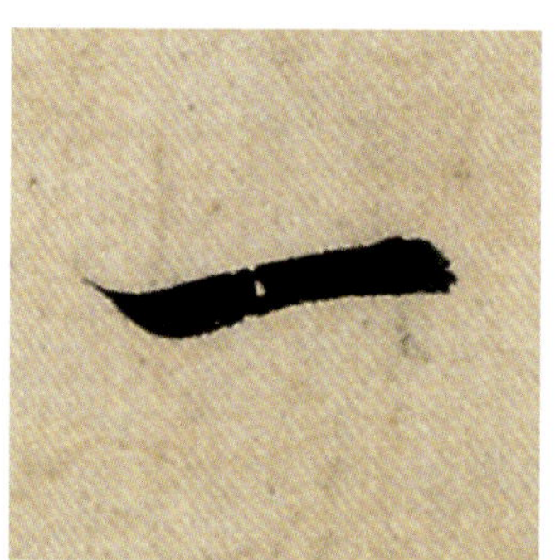

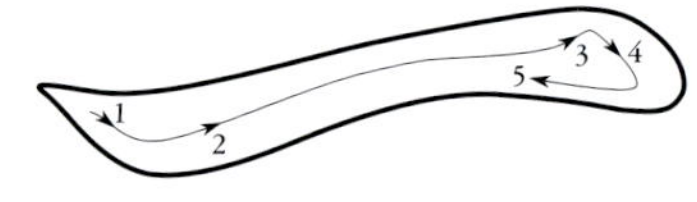

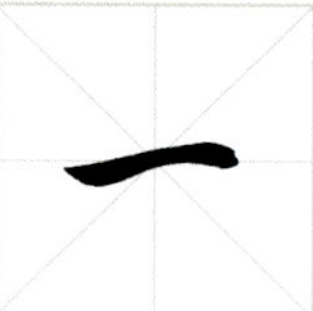

Example: 一 **(One)**

(1) Begin the stroke with the brush tip going towards the right, and then gently press the brush tip down in the lower right direction;
(2) Lift the brush slightly, move the brush tip from along the side to the middle, and wield the brush to the right with effort;
(3) Lift the brush slightly in the upper right direction;
(4) Press the brush down in the lower right direction;
(5) When ending the stroke, lift the right wrist gently and quickly make a hook-like movement towards the reverse direction. Sometimes, the stroke is followed with a puller that triggers off the next stroke.

Short Horizontal

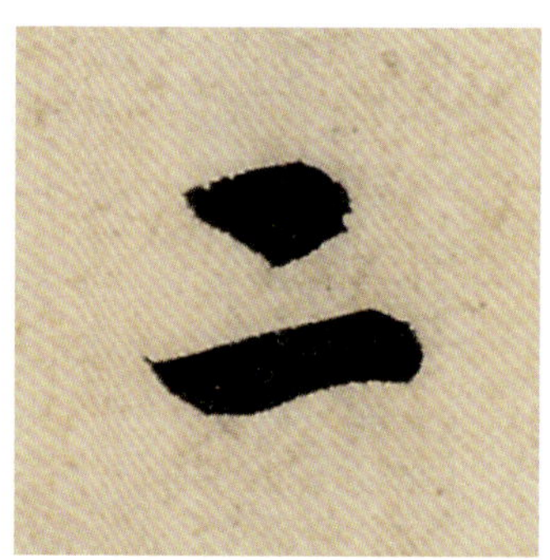

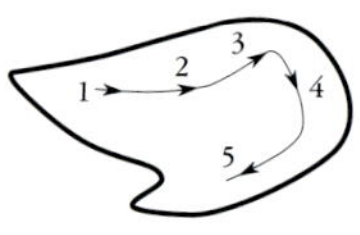

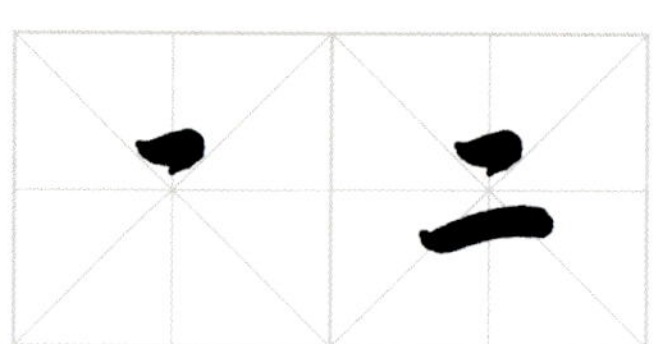

Example: 二 **(Two)**

(1) Begin the stroke with the brush tip going towards the right, and then gently press the brush tip down in the lower right direction;
(2) Lift the brush slightly, move the brush tip from along the side to the middle;
(3) Lift the brush slightly in the upper right direction;
(4) Press the brush down in the lower right direction;
(5) Bend the brush tip to the lower left and start the next stroke with a puller.

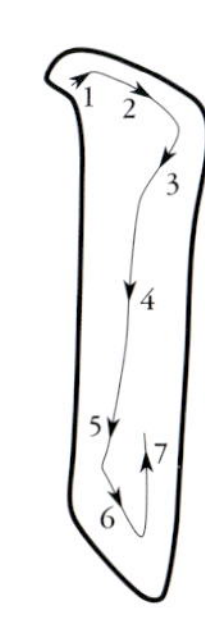

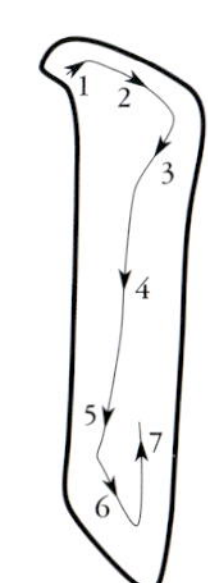

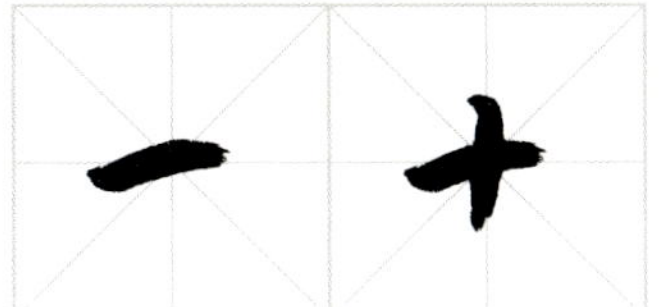

Straight Vertical Stroke

Example: 十 (Ten)

(1) Make an upward hook-like movement to start the stroke;

(2) Bend the brush tip and press it down in the lower right direction;

(3) Move the brush slightly towards the left and then wield the brush tip from along the side to the middle;

(4) Move the brush downwards, keeping the brush tip in the middle;

(5) Lift the brush slightly;

(6) Press the brush down in the lower right direction;

(7) Make an upward hook-like movement at the end of the stroke

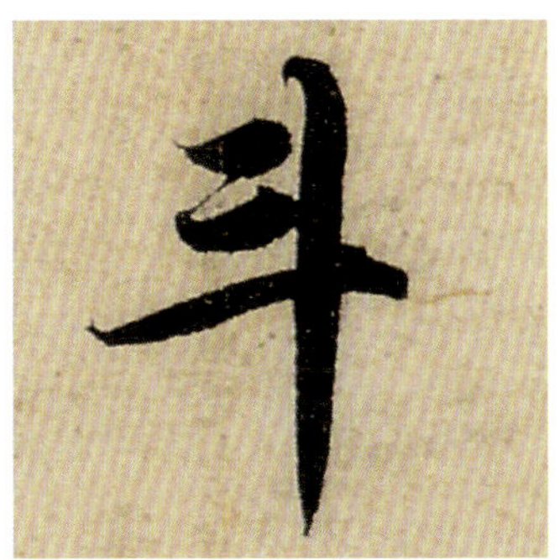

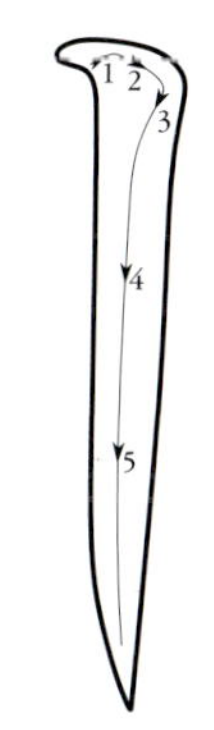

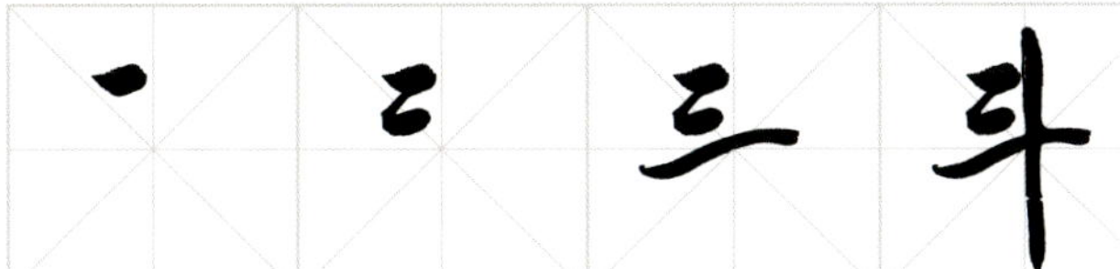

Hanging Vertical Stroke

Example: 斗 (Fight)

(1) Make an upward hook-like movement to start the stroke;

(2) Bend the brush tip and press it down in the lower right direction;

(3) Move the brush slightly towards the left and then wield the brush tip from along the side to the middle;

(4) Move the brush downwards, keeping the brush tip in the middle;

(5) Gradually lift the brush while it is being wielded, until the brush tip moves away from the paper.

Horizontal Stroke with a Vertical Turn

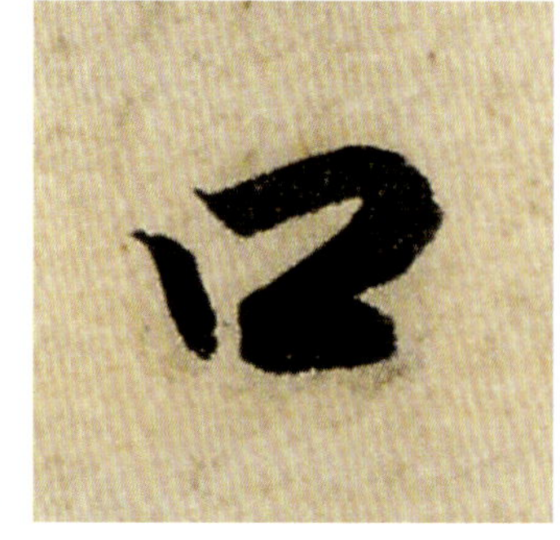

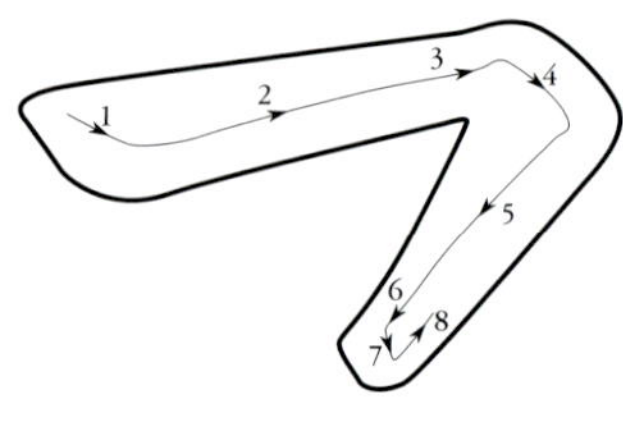

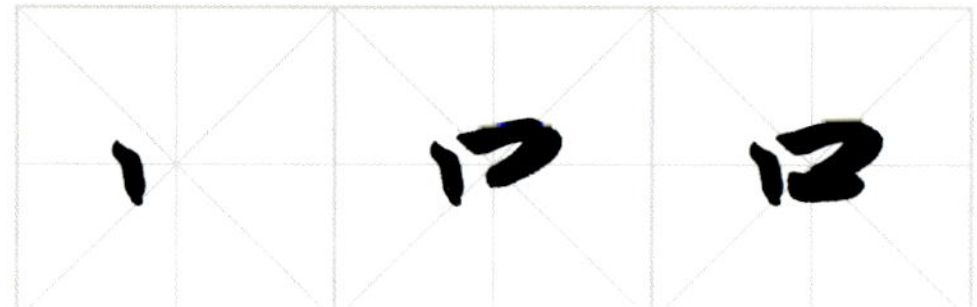

Example: 口 (Mouth)

(1) Begin the stroke with the brush tip going towards the right, and then gently press the brush tip down in the lower right direction;
(2) Lift the brush slightly, move the brush tip from along the side to the middle, and then wield the brush towards the right;
(3) Lift the brush slightly;
(4) Press the brush down in the lower right direction;
(5) Move the brush tip from along the side to the middle, and then wield the brush downwards;
(6) Lift the brush slightly;
(7) Press the brush down in the lower right direction;
(8) Make a hook-like movement at the end of the stroke.

Upper Dot Stroke

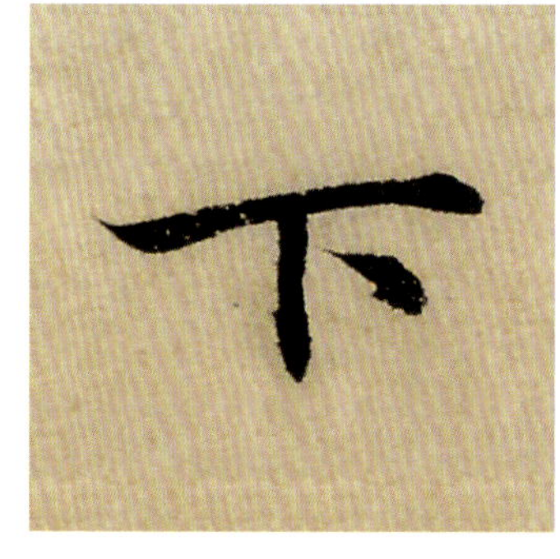

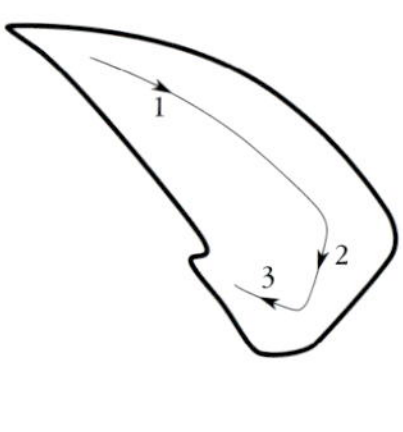

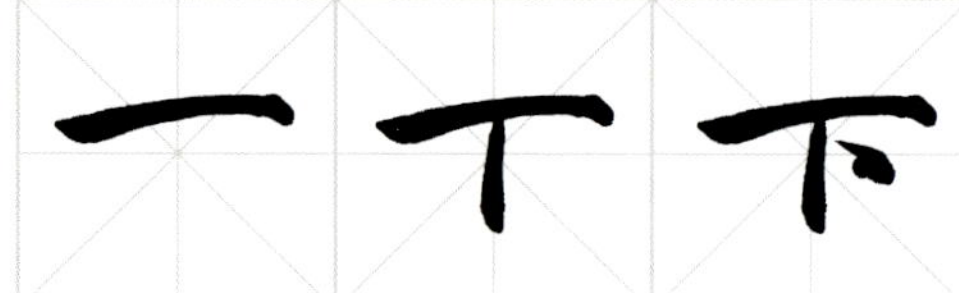

Example: 下 (Down)

(1) Begin the stroke with the brush tip going downwards, and then press the brush tip down in the lower right direction;
(2) Lift the brush;
(3) Move the brush tip in the lower left direction.

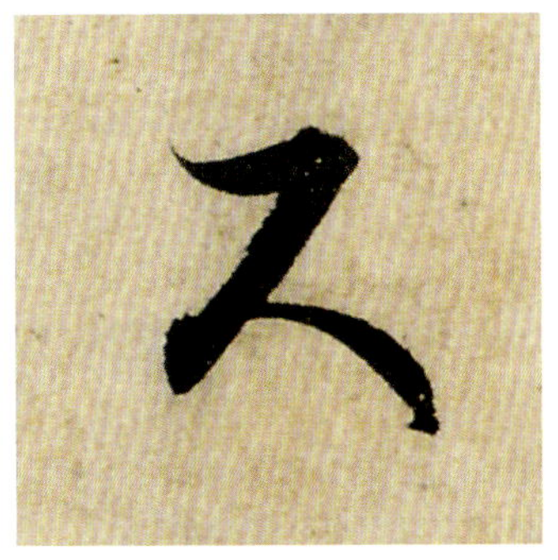

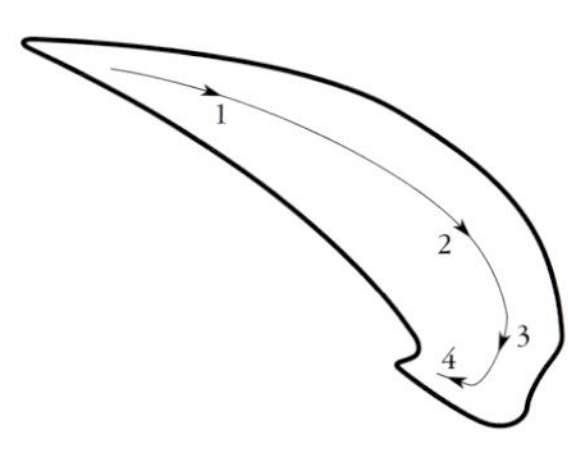

Long Dot

Example: 乂 (In ancient times, 尺 which means ruler is often written as 乂 in semi-cursive script.)

(1) Begin the stroke with the brush tip going downwards, and move the brush down towards the right in an arch;

(2) Gradually press the brush in the lower right direction;

(3) Lift the brush;

(4) End the stroke by moving the brush in the lower left direction.

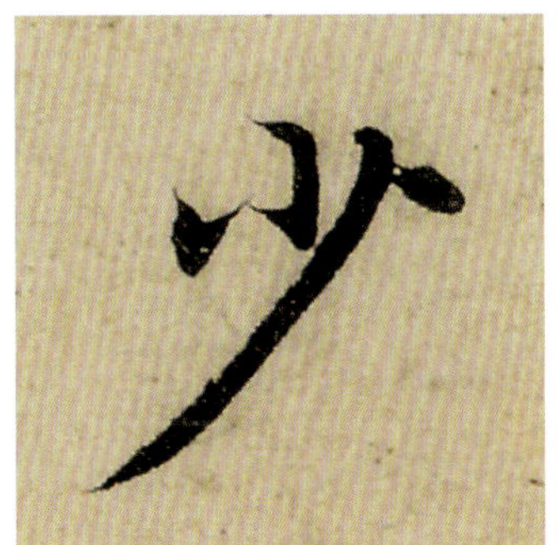

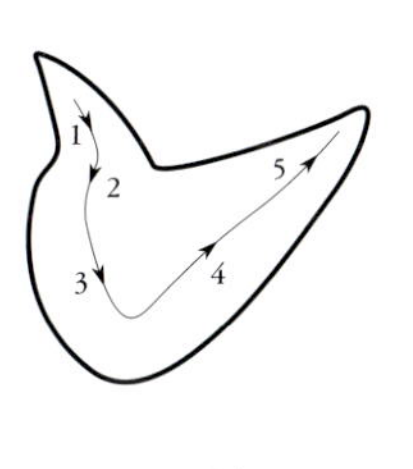

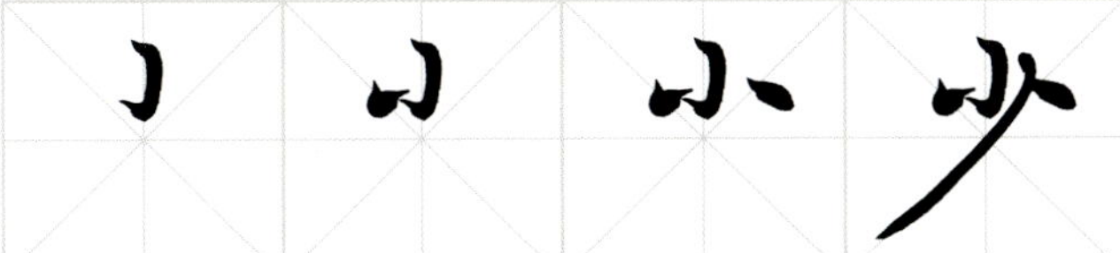

Lower Right Dot

Example: 少 (Less)

(1) Begin the stroke from top to bottom with the brush tip going downwards, and press down the brush, first lightly and then heavily;

(2) Lift the brush;

(3) Slightly press the brush down in the lower right direction;

(4) Wield the brush in the upper right direction, moving the brush tip from sidelong to the middle;

(5) Raise the brush in the upper right direction.

Upstroke to the Right

Example: 江 (River)

(1) Begin the stroke from top to bottom with the brush tip going downwards, and then press the brush down;
(2) Lift the brush, move the brush tip to the middle, and press the brush down;
(3) Lift the brush gradually.

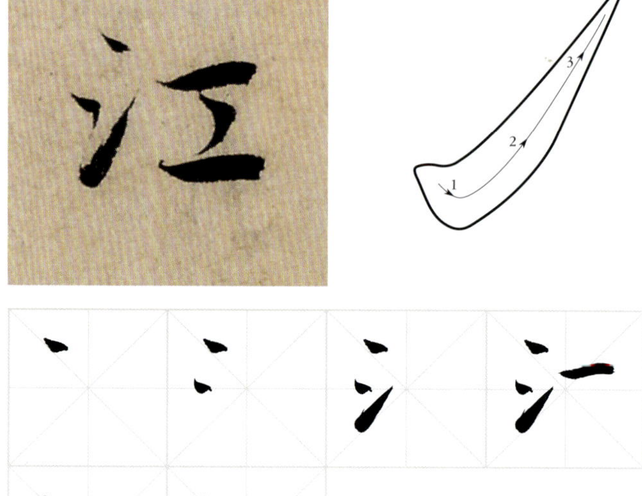

Vertical Hooked Stroke

Example: 長 (Traditional Chinese character of 长, long)

(1) Begin the stroke with the brush tip going downwards, and then press the brush down;
(2) Lift the brush and move the brush tip to the middle;
(3) Move the brush downward, keeping the brush tip in the middle;
(4) Lift the brush;
(5) Press the brush tip down in the lower right direction;
(6) Move the brush tip in the middle;
(7) Press the brush down slightly;
(8) Move the brush in an arch;
(9) End the stroke gradually.

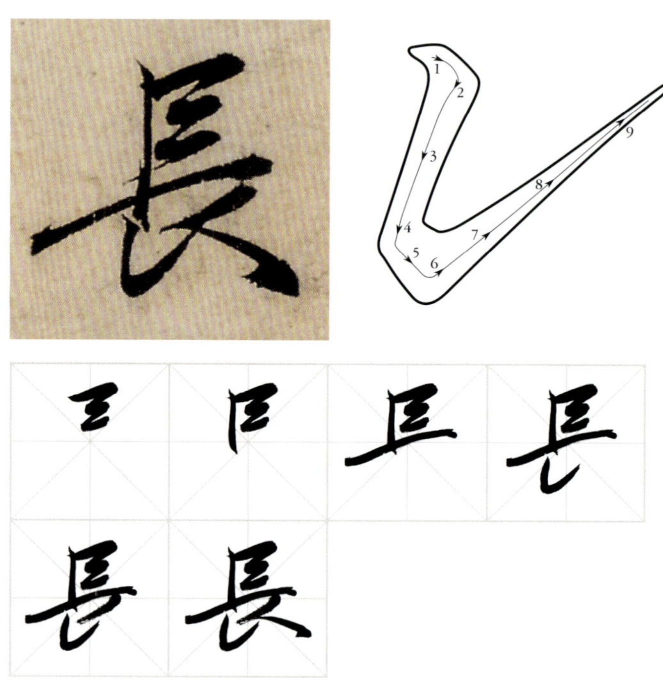

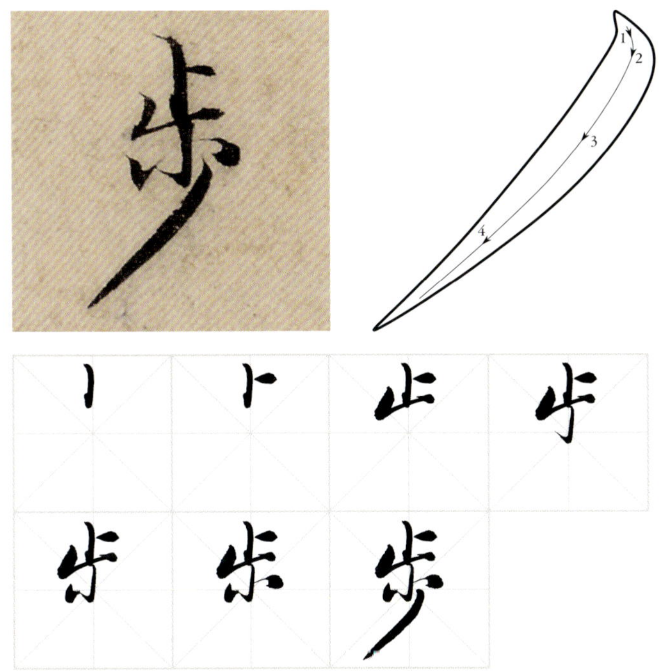

Long Downward Left Curved Stroke

Example: 步 (Step)

(1) Begin the stroke from the upper left to the lower right with the brush tip going towards the left, and then press the brush down;

(2) Move the brush slightly with the brush tip in the middle;

(3) Move the brush downwards in an arch, keeping the brush tip in the middle;

(4) End the stroke gradually in the lower left direction.

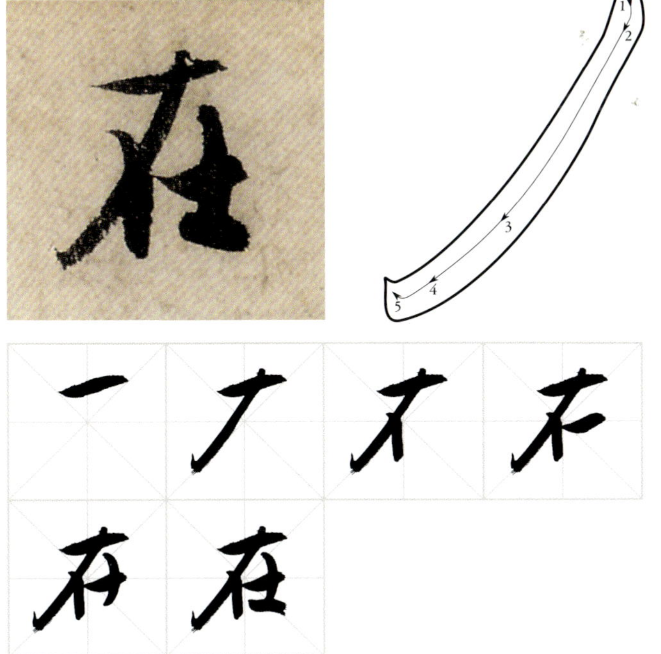

Downward Left Curved Stroke

Example: 在 (At)

(1) Begin the stroke with the brush tip going towards the left;

(2) Move the brush tip in the middle;

(3) Move the brush downwards in an arch, keeping the brush tip in the middle;

(4) Lift the brush slightly;

(5) Make a hook-like movement in the upper left direction at the end of the stroke.

Short Downward Left Curved Stroke

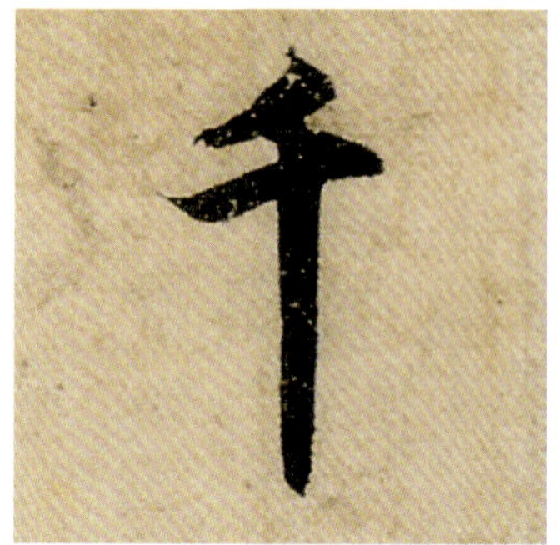

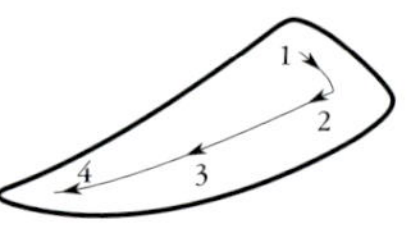

Example: 千 (Thousand)

(1) Begin the stroke from the upper left to the lower right with the brush tip going towards the left, and then press the brush down;
(2) Move the brush tip to the middle;
(3) Slightly press the brush down;
(4) End the stroke gradually in the lower left direction.

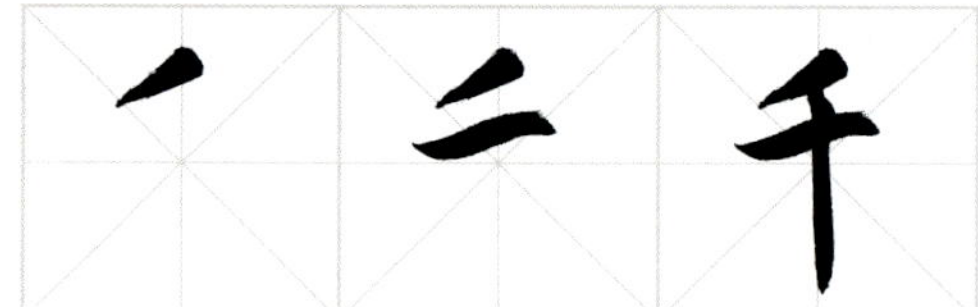

Downwards Right Concave Stroke

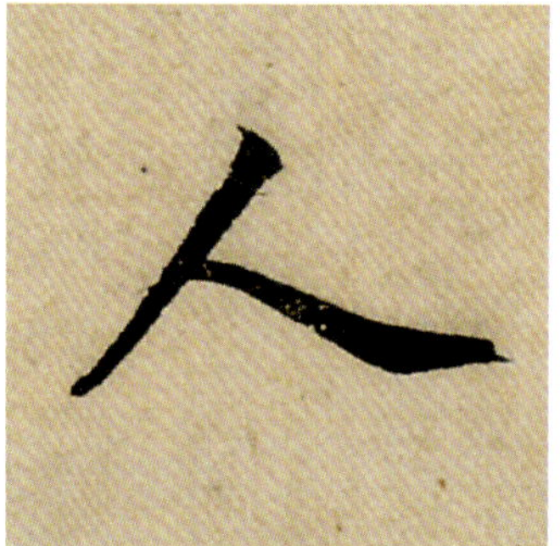

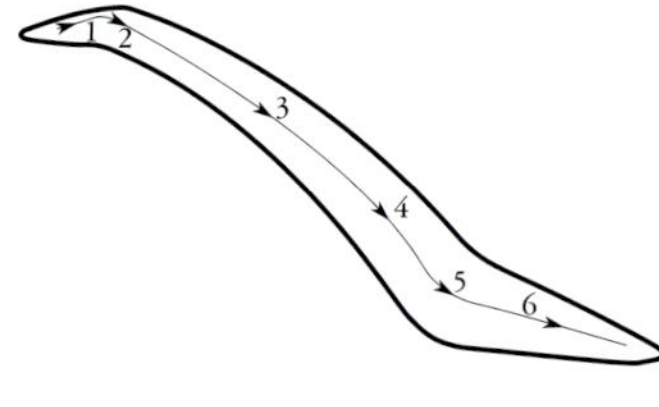

Example: 人 (People)

(1) Begin the stroke from left to right with the brush tip going towards the right, and then press the brush down;
(2) Bend the brush, press it down, and move it upwards;
(3) Move the brush downwards in a slight arch, keeping the brush tip in the middle;
(4) Press the brush in the lower right direction gradually;
(5) Move the brush towards the right;
(6) End the stroke by lifting the brush gradually towards its right movement.

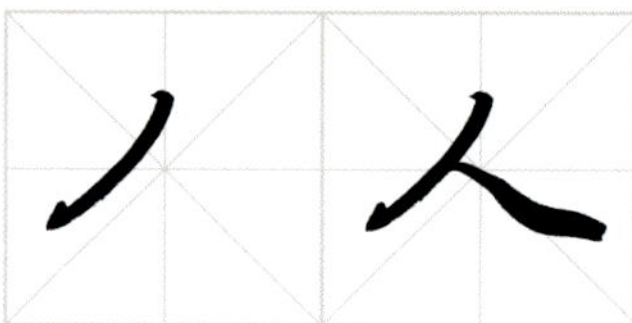

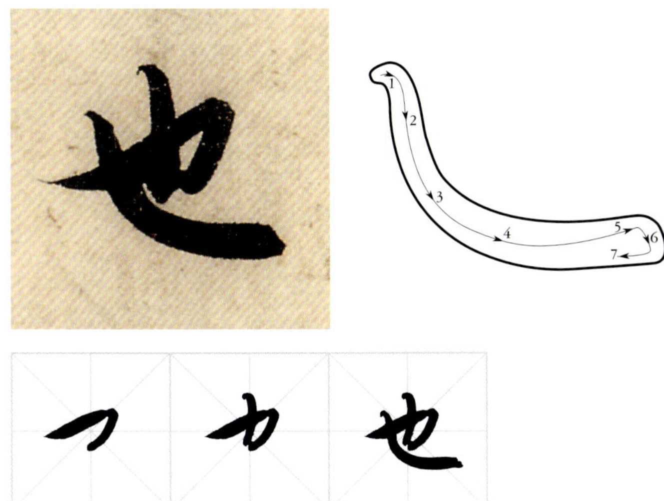

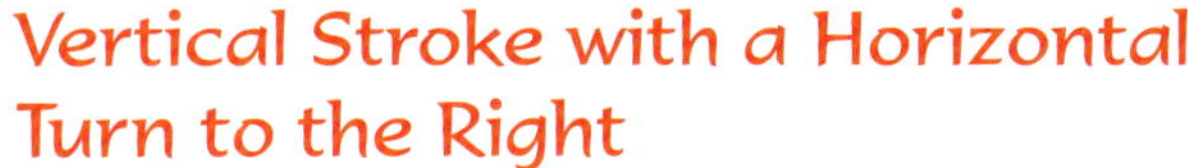

Vertical Stroke with a Horizontal Turn to the Right

Example: 也 (Also)

(1) Begin the stroke from the upper left to the lower right with the brush tip going downwards, and slightly press the brush down;
(2) Move the brush downwards in an arch, keeping the brush tip in the middle;
(3) Lift the brush and turn the wrist towards the right;
(4) Move the brush towards the right in an arch;
(5) Lift the brush;
(6) Press the brush in the lower right direction;
(7) Make a hook-like movement towards the left at the end of the stroke.

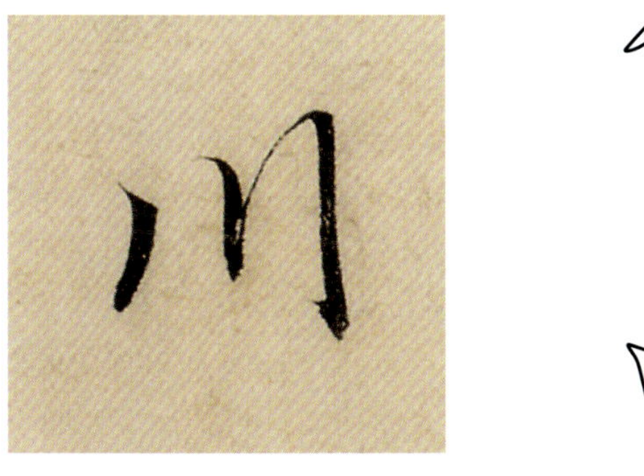

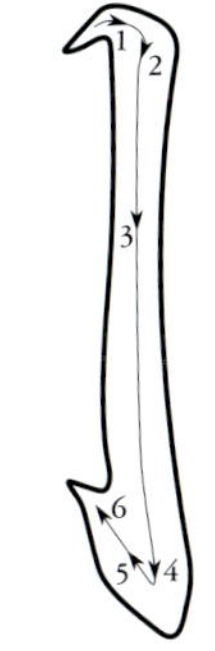

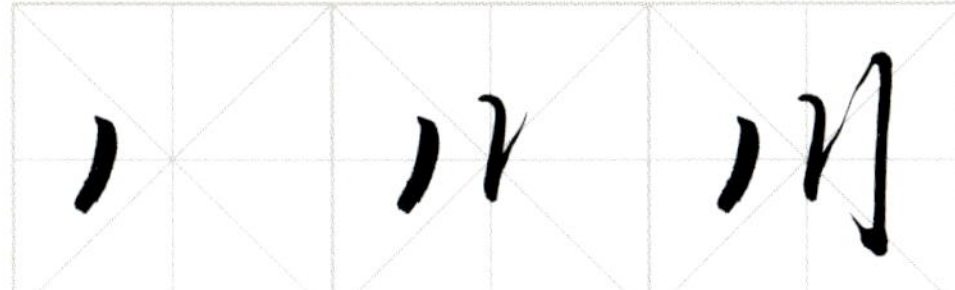

Vertical Stroke with a Hook

Example: 川 (River)

(1) Begin the stroke from left to right with the brush tip going towards the right, and then press the brush down;
(2) Move the brush tip to the middle;
(3) Move the brush downwards;
(4) Lift the brush, and move the brush tip to the middle;
(5) Slightly press down the brush;
(6) Make a hook towards the left, with the brush tip reaching the end of the hook.

Horizontal Stroke with a Downward Turn and a Hook

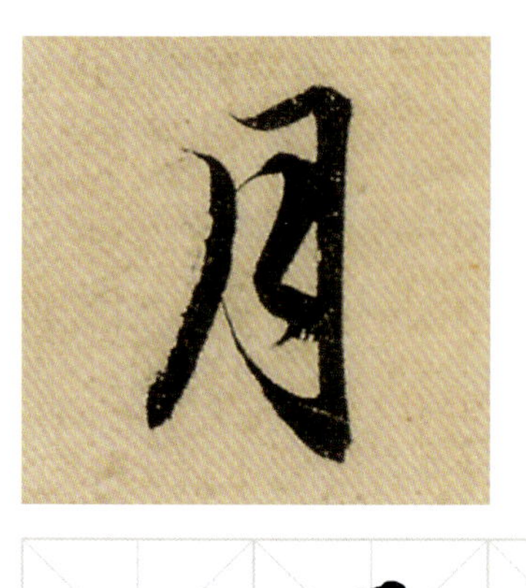

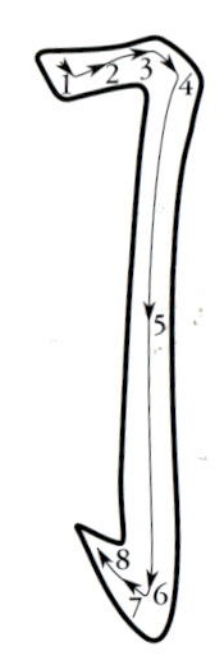

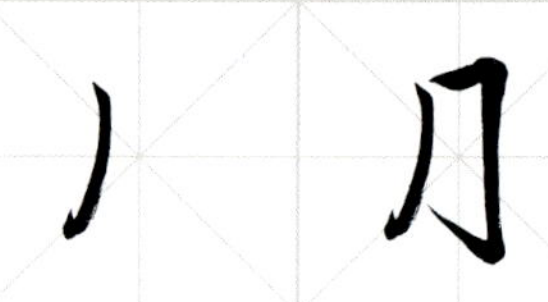

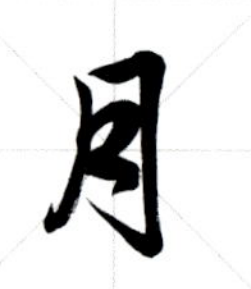

Example: 月 (Moon)

(1) Begin the stroke with the brush tip going towards the right, and press the brush down in the lower right direction;
(2) Lift the brush slightly, move the brush tip from along the side to the middle, and then continue the brush towards the right;
(3) Lift the brush slightly in the upper right direction;
(4) Press the brush down in the lower right direction;
(5) Move the brush tip from along the side to the middle, and then continue the brush downwards;
(6) Lift the brush and move the brush tip to the middle;
(7) Slightly press the brush down;
(8) Make a hook towards the left, with the brush tip reaching the end of the hook.

Flat Hook Stroke

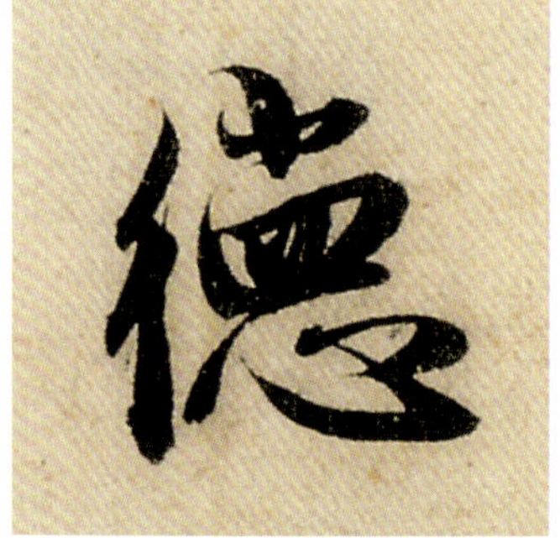

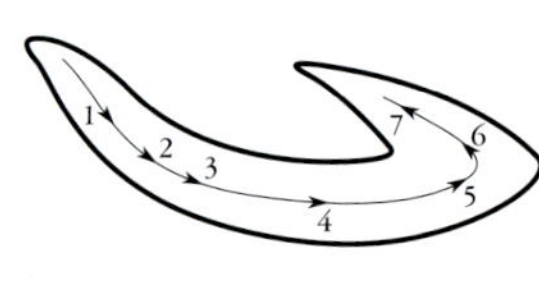

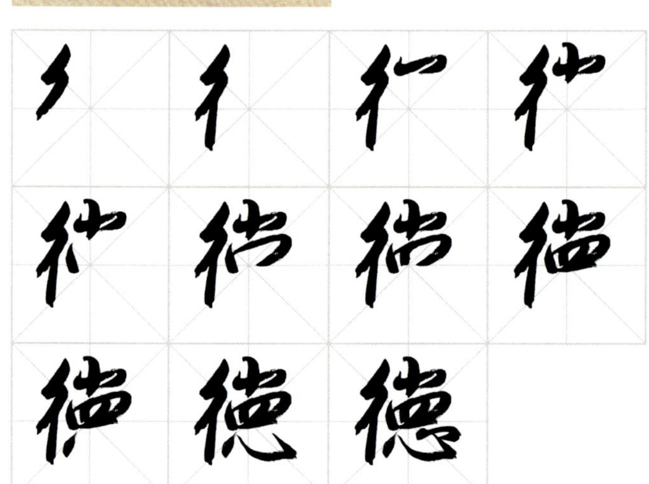

Example: 德 (Virtue)

(1) Begin the stroke in the lower right direction, with the brush tip going towards the right, and then press the brush down;
(2) Lift the brush slightly, and move it towards the right with effort;
(3) Lift the brush and move the brush tip to the middle;
(4) Press the brush down in the lower right direction;
(5) Wield the brush back towards the left, and then move the brush tip towards the right;
(6) Move the brush tip back towards the left and then straighten out the brush;
(7) Wield the brush in the upper left direction, with the brush tip reaching the end of the hook.

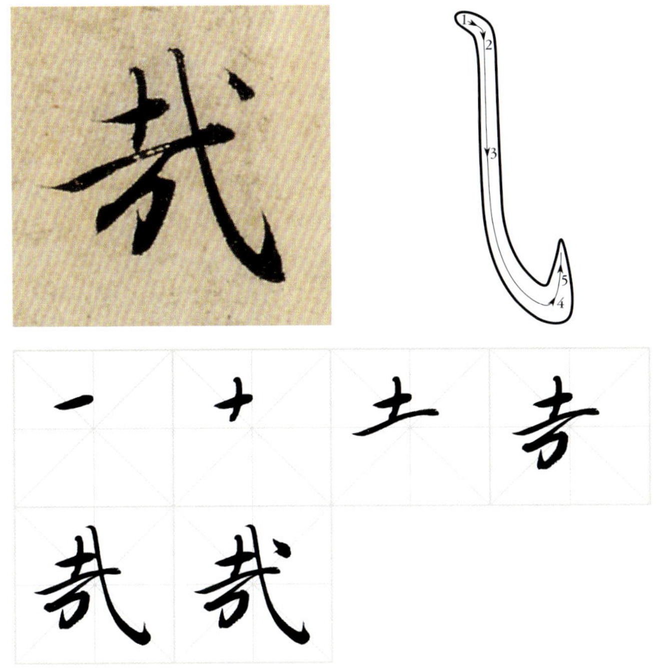

Hooked Arc Stroke

Example: 茙 (In ancient times, 哉 which means indeed is written as 茙 in semi-cursive script.)

(1) Begin the stroke with the brush tip going towards the right, and press the brush down in the lower right direction;
(2) Lift the brush slightly and move the brush tip from along the side to the middle;
(3) Wield the brush in the lower right direction with effort;
(4) Move the brush tip back upwards;
(5) Follow the momentum to end the stroke, with the brush tip reaching the end of the hook.

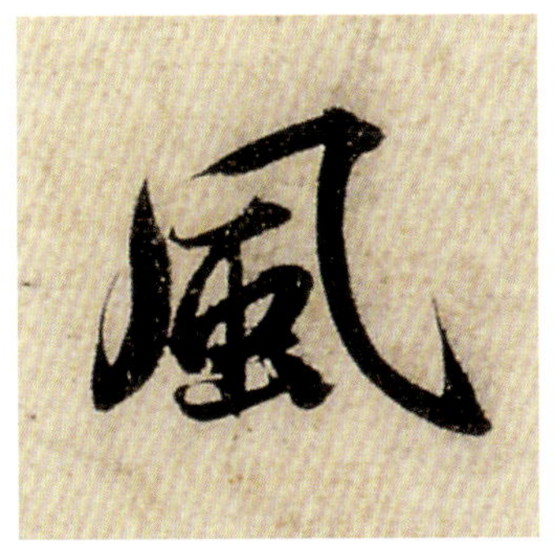

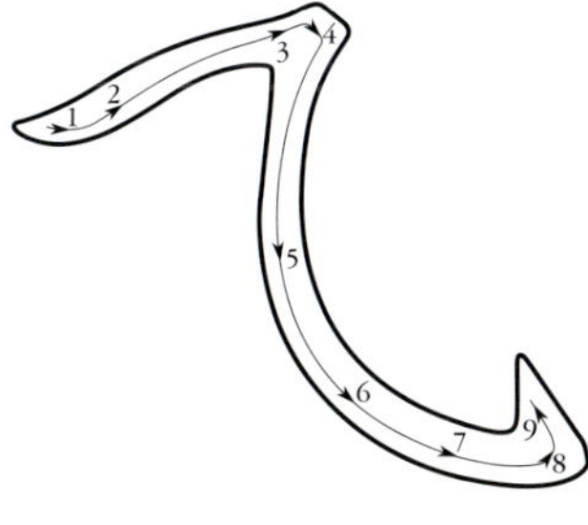

Horizontal Stroke with a Downward Turn, then a Right Turn and a Hook

Example: 風 (Traditional Chinese character of 风 , wind)

(1) Begin the stroke with the brush tip going towards the right, and press the brush down in the lower right direction;
(2) Lift the brush slightly, move the brush tip from along the side to the middle, and then wield the brush towards the right with effort;
(3) Lift the brush slightly in the upper right direction;
(4) Press the brush down in the lower right direction;
(5) Move the brush tip from along the side to the middle, and then continue the brush downwards in an arch;
(6) Lift the brush slightly, move the brush tip from along the side to the middle;
(7) Wield the brush in the lower right direction with effort;
(8) Move the brush tip back upwards;
(9) Follow the momentum to end the stroke, with the brush tip reaching the end of the hook.

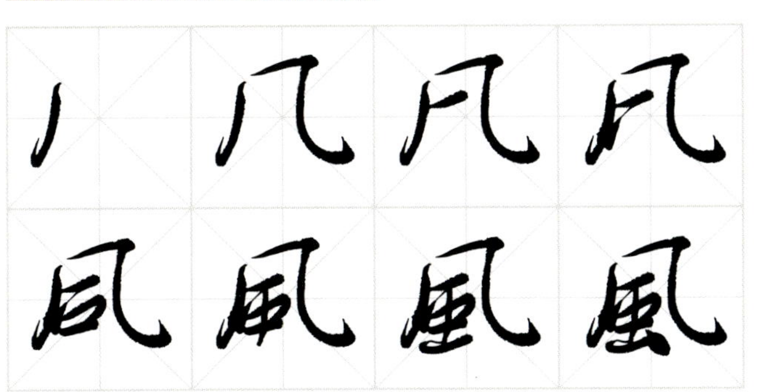

2. Combined Strokes

Unlike regular script, semi-cursive script is often written naturally and smoothly in one go and between strokes, there usually appear connections and pullers. Some of the strokes may link naturally, while others, though physically separated, show internal connections. Therefore, a good knowledge of combined strokes is essential for beginners of calligraphy.

Puller of Horizontal and Vertical Strokes in One Character

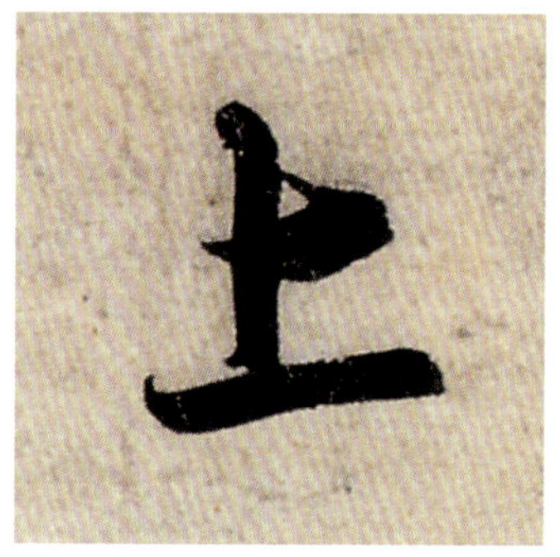

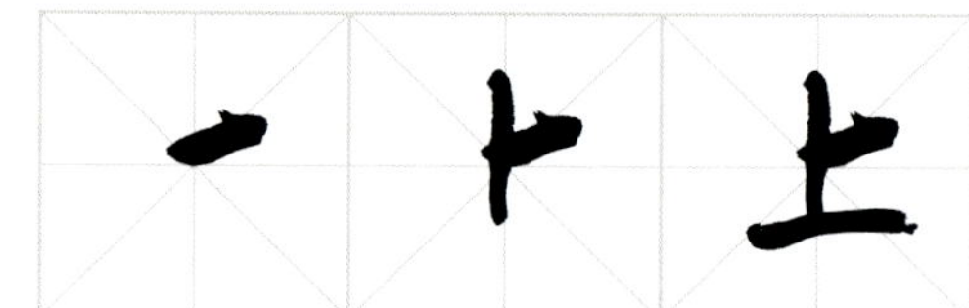

Example: 上 (Up)

(1) Begin the stroke with the brush tip going the direction intended, move the brush tip to the middle, and wield the brush in the upper right direction;
(2) Lift the brush in the upper left direction;
(3) Move the brush tip to the middle and then slightly press the brush down;
(4) Wield the brush downwards, keeping the brush tip in the middle;
(5) Lift the brush in the lower left direction;
(6) Lift the brush;
(7) Move the brush first lightly and then heavily, and slightly press it down;
(8) Move the brush tip to the middle, and wield the brush in the upper right direction;
(9) Lift the brush and then press it down in the lower right direction;
(10) Make a hook-like movement of the brush at the end of a stroke.

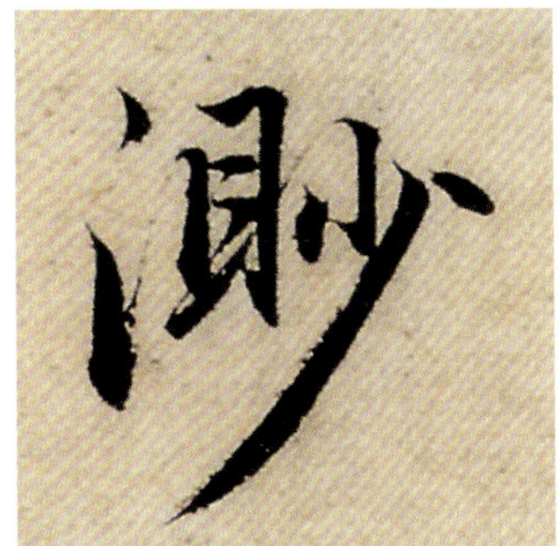

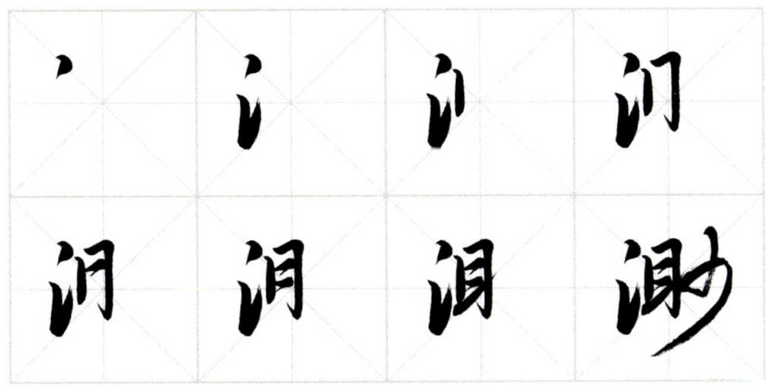

Three-Dot Water

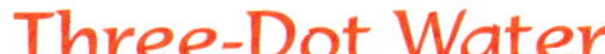

Example: 渺 **(Tiny)**

(1) Begin the stroke with the brush tip going towards the right, and then press the brush down gently;
(2) Lift the brush;
(3) Raise the brush in the lower left direction;
(4) Follow the momentum and press down the brush in the lower right direction, and move the brush downwards, keeping the brush tip in the middle;
(5) Lift the brush;
(6) Press the brush down in the lower right direction;
(7) Move the brush tip to the middle, follow the momentum and raise the brush in the upper right direction, and start the next stroke at the same time.

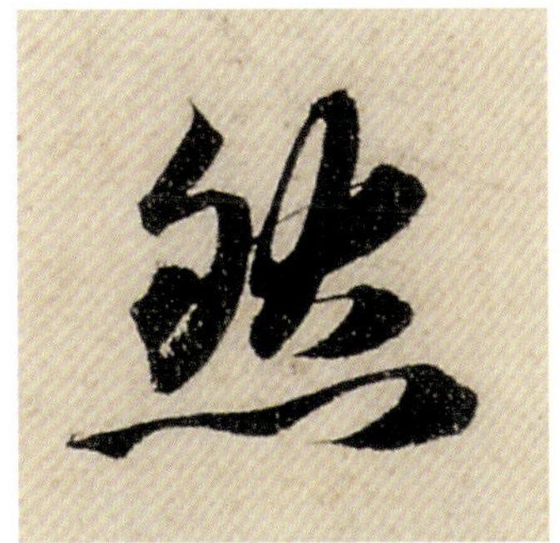

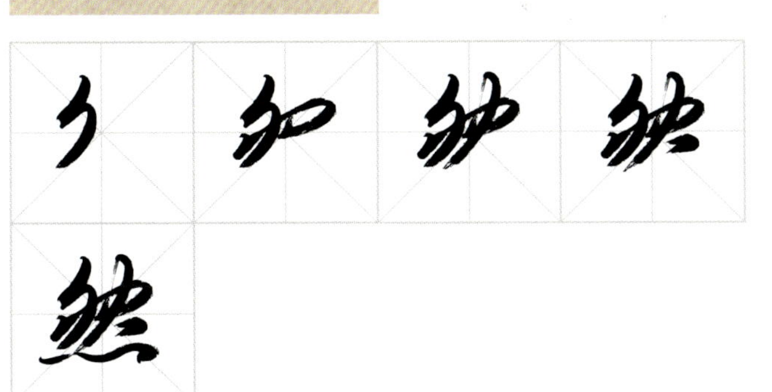

A Group of Four Dots at the Bottom

Example: 然 **(So)**

(1) Begin the stroke with the brush tip going towards the right, and then press the brush down gently;
(2) Lift the brush in the upper right direction, but keep the brush tip on the paper;
(3) Press the brush down again;
(4) Lift the brush in the upper right direction again, and keep the brush tip on the paper;
(5) Press the brush down in the lower right direction;
(6) Move the brush tip to the middle and raise the brush in the lower left direction.

Puller of Multi-horizontal Strokes in One Character

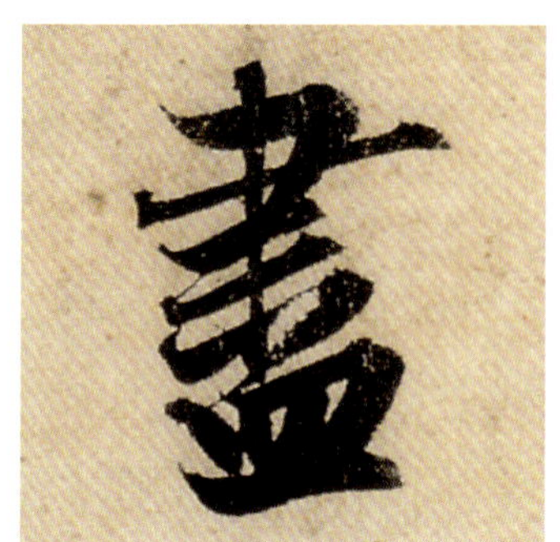

Example: 盡 (Traditional Chinese character of 尽, all)

At the end of each stroke, the puller, physically existent or non-existent, will start the next stroke. The writer needs to focus on the direction of and changes in each horizontal stroke.

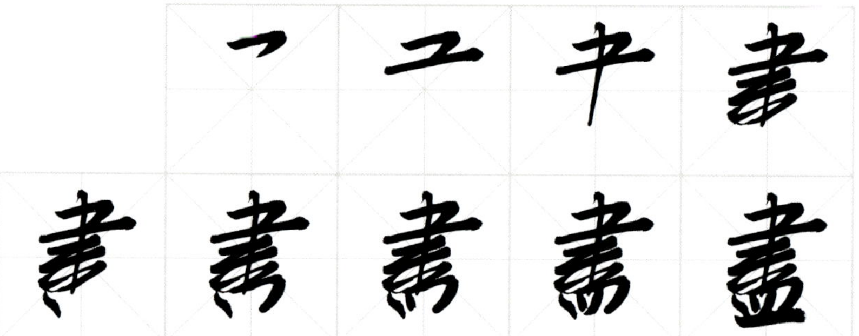

Puller of Multi-vertical Strokes in One Character

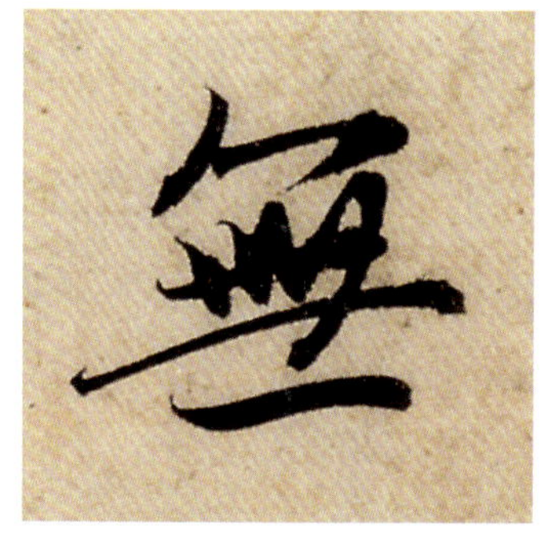

Example: 無 (Traditional Chinese character of 无, all)

At the end of each stroke, the puller, physically existent or non-existent, will start the next stroke. The writer needs to focus on the direction of and changes in each vertical stroke.

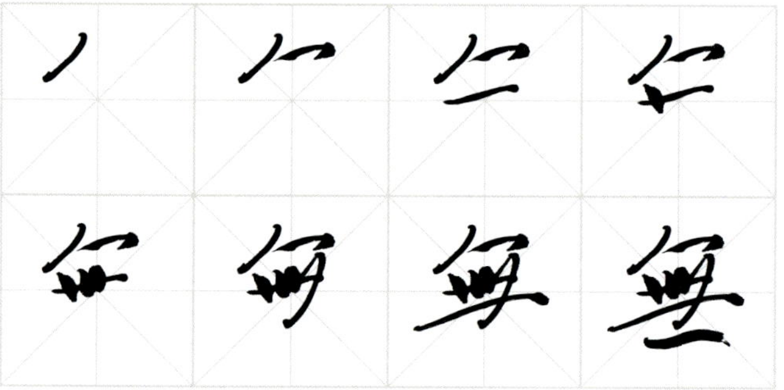

3. Spatial Structures of Chinese Characters

The spatial structure of a character reflects the basic formation of calligraphy, i.e. the proper arrangement of a specific stroke in a character for maximum beauty, the ideal separation of a character by the strokes that constitute it for harmony of space. The spatial structure of the character, along with character strokes and the art of character composition, is known as the three basic factors of calligraphy. The spatial structure of the character in regular script is relatively regular; however, it is highly varied in semi-cursive script. Therefore, exercises in the spatial structures of characters will enable the learners to command the basic laws governing changes in the spatial structures of semi-cursive script.

Compromise in Space between the Right and Left Parts of a Character

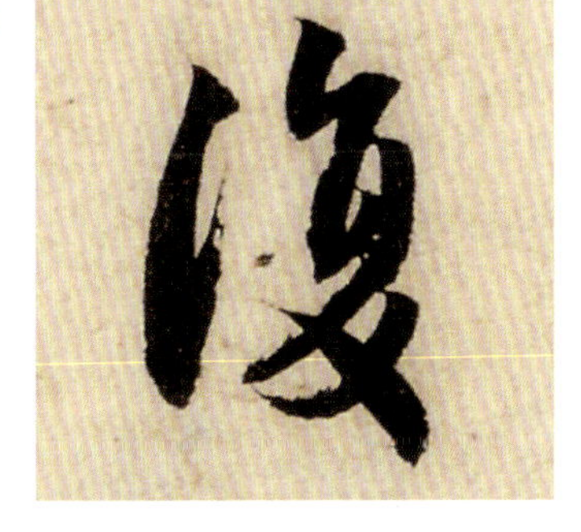

Example: 復 (Traditional Chinese character of 复, again)

The right and left parts of a character need to make a compromise in space to form spatial structures that are both dependent and independent of each other. This is an aesthetic rule used extensively in calligraphy. Take the character 復 as an example. The left part inclines to the left, leaving space for a rising stroke at the end of the two-person stroke. The rising stroke, in turn, triggers off the left-falling stroke on the right. The right part of the character slants to the right to avoid collision with the rising stroke in the middle. The whole character shows good harmony in changes. Making compromises is an aesthetic pursuit that has its origin in humility, a virtue in traditional Chinese culture.

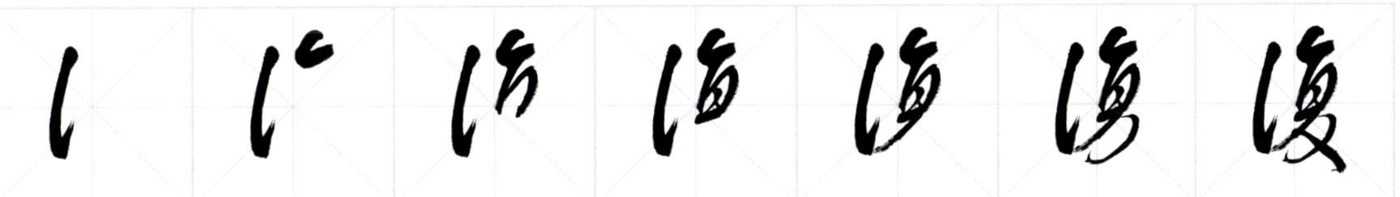

Princess and Porter Vying for Passage

One day, Zhang Xu (675 – 750?), a famous calligrapher in the Tang Dynasty, saw that a parade of people carrying the princess in a sedan chair were scrambling for passage with a porter on a narrow road, and neither was willing to give ground. This put both sides in a dilemma. In the end, only when the porter moved to the left side of the road and the parade to the right side did they pass the road successfully. This observation offered the calligrapher some enlightenment: beauty of harmony in calligraphy can be achieved only when compromise is made between different lines of characters and between the right and left parts of a single character. This was later developed into a rule of aesthetics in calligraphy.

Right and Left Parts of the Character in Picturesque Disorder

Example: 動 (Traditional Chinese character of 动, move)

For characters with a left-right structure, the right and left parts should be in picturesque disorder.

Chinese characters are based on pictographs that follow the law of nature. This has much to do with the environment Chinese forefathers lived in. They mostly lived near mountains and by rivers and what they saw, heard, and felt were mainly the sun, the moon, stars, mountains, rivers, flowers, birds, insects, and fish. So they would naturally integrate their images into the characters they invented.

Chinese calligraphy is the art of writing Chinese characters. It is the feelings and wisdom of calligraphers that enhance the beauty of Chinese characters. They apply the law of natural beauty they have discovered to their aesthetic appreciation, making their calligraphic works natural, lifelike, and dynamic. For example, a character with a left-right structure often looks exactly like two adjacent mountains with endless undulations in picturesque disorder.

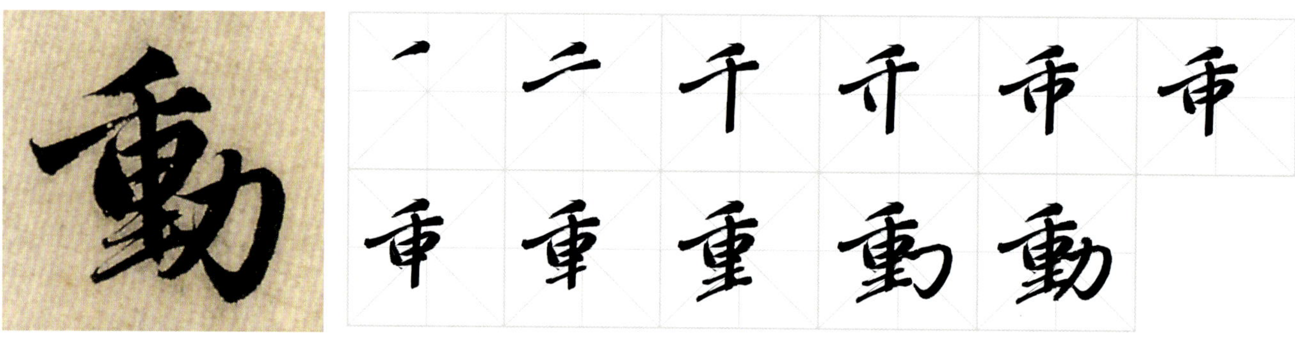

Alternating between What Is Real and What Is Virtual

Example: 周 (Week)

Pullers and connections often link character strokes in semi-cursive script. The strokes are real, while the pullers and connections are often virtual. Some of the connecting actions are even accomplished above the paper in the air. However, though the strokes may be physically separated, they show strong internal connections.

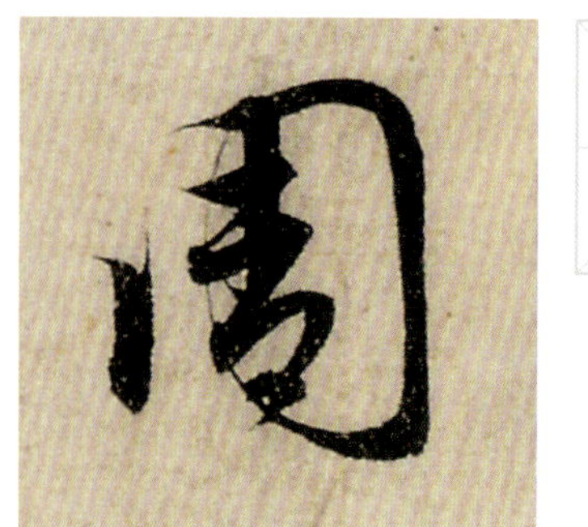

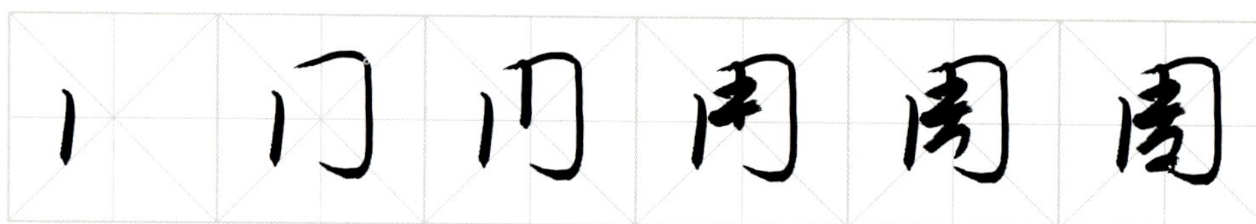

The Bottom Bearing the Top

Example: 遊 (Ttaditional Chinese character of 游, swim)

Characters of this kind often have a bottom part that is steady and often long and thick, which props up the top part of the character. Such characters often have a top-bottom structure, like 遊 (walk or travel), 孟 (a surname), and 想 (think). They look exactly like the Temple of Heaven in Beijing, which, looking from a distance, connects heaven and earth and is dignified and magnificent.

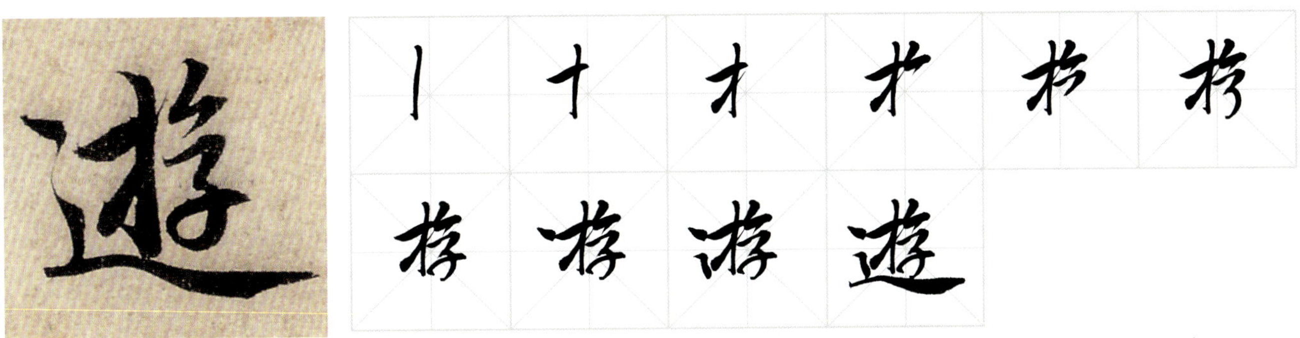

The Top Covering the Bottom

Example: 今 (Today)

Characters with a top-bottom structure, such as 今 (today), 家 (family), and 穿 (wear), are always bigger at the top, which covers the bottom part of the character like the heaven shrouding the earth. This kind of calligraphic structure matches in beauty of the unique Chinese architectural structure.

The China Pavilion at the World Exposition, Shanghai, is reputed to be "the Crown of the East." With the lower part shrouded by the top, it is a fine display of the spirit and temperament of Chinese culture.

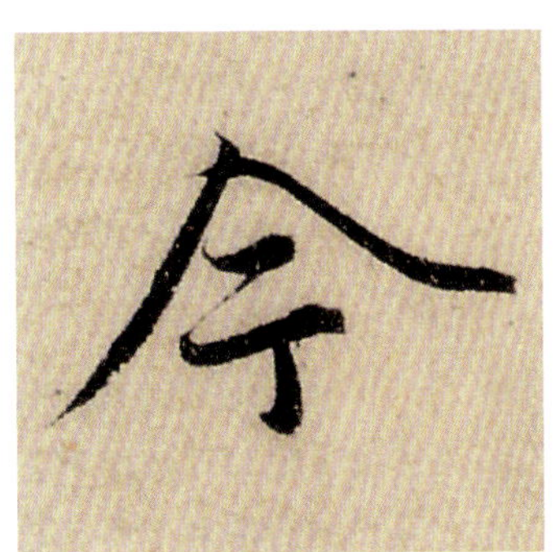

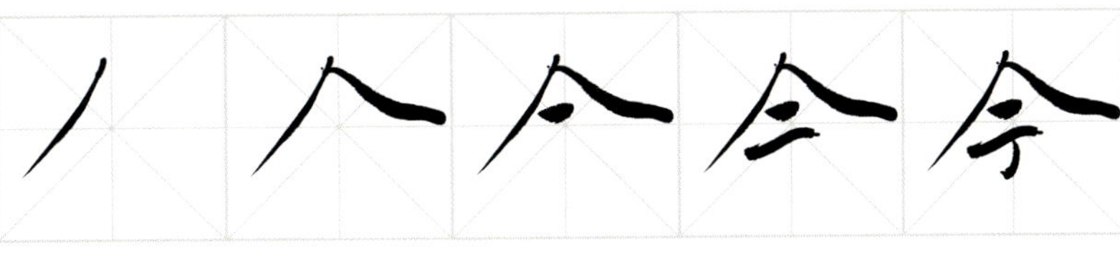

4. Composition of Calligraphy and Ancient Calligraphic Work Copying

The calligraphic work emphasizes the echo between strokes, the harmony between characters, and the lines setting off each other. Only in this way can the whole work have a free-flowing momentum and a balanced composition.

The composition of calligraphy refers to the overall layout of a calligraphic work. Normally, a calligraphic work is written in vertical lines from right to left. The vertical direction is known as the line and the horizontal direction as the row. In regular and clerical scripts, the line and row are often brought into alignment and the intervals between characters are often the same. In semi-cursive script, the lines are justified, but not the rows, and in each row there are characters that are bigger or smaller, straight or slanted. In cursive script, both the lines and rows are unjustified, the characters vary in size, and the distance between lines keeps changing, presenting a scene of natural and unrestrained beauty and reminding the viewers of the poetic line "pearls, big and small, falling into a jade plate."

The most common forms of calligraphic composition are horizontally hung scrolls, central scrolls (hanging in the middle of the wall of the main room), fan coverings, and couplets.

Horizontally Hung Scroll: A relatively common form of calligraphy.

Examples: 中和

The characters 中 (*zhong*, middle) and 和 (*he*, harmony) means all creatures under heaven get what they want and live in harmonious coexistence.

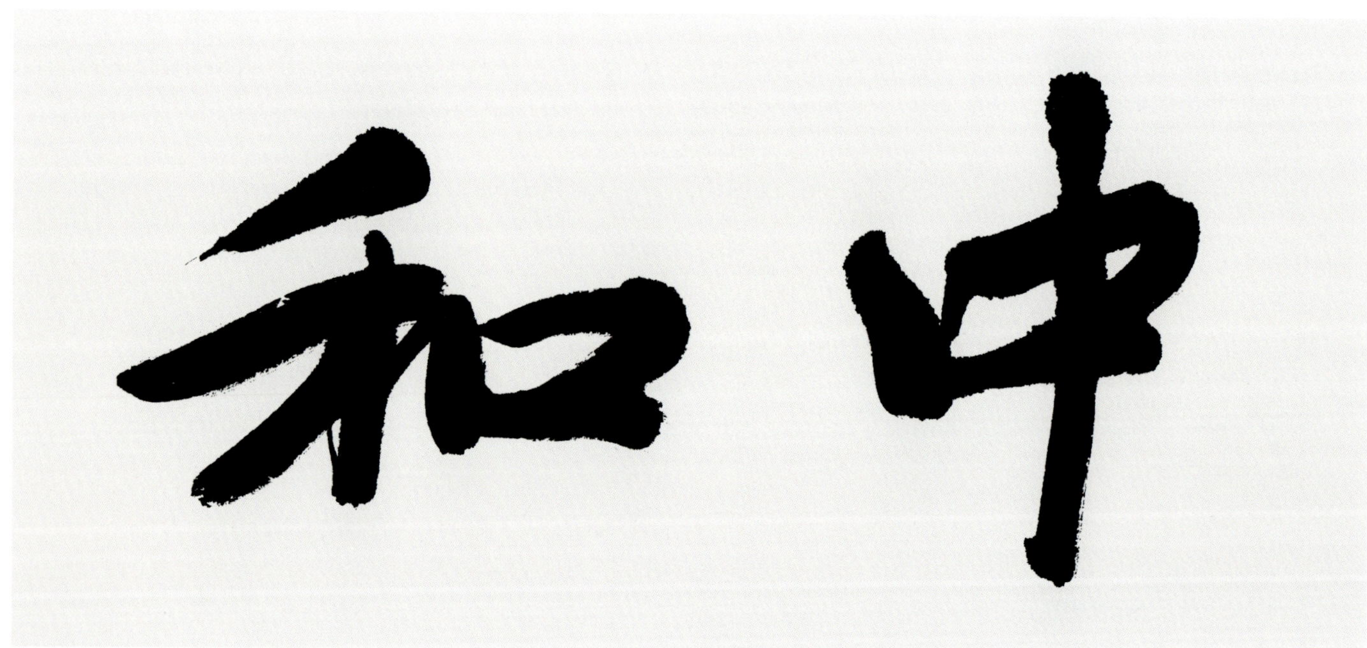

Central Scroll: A form of calligraphy hung in the middle of the wall of the main room.

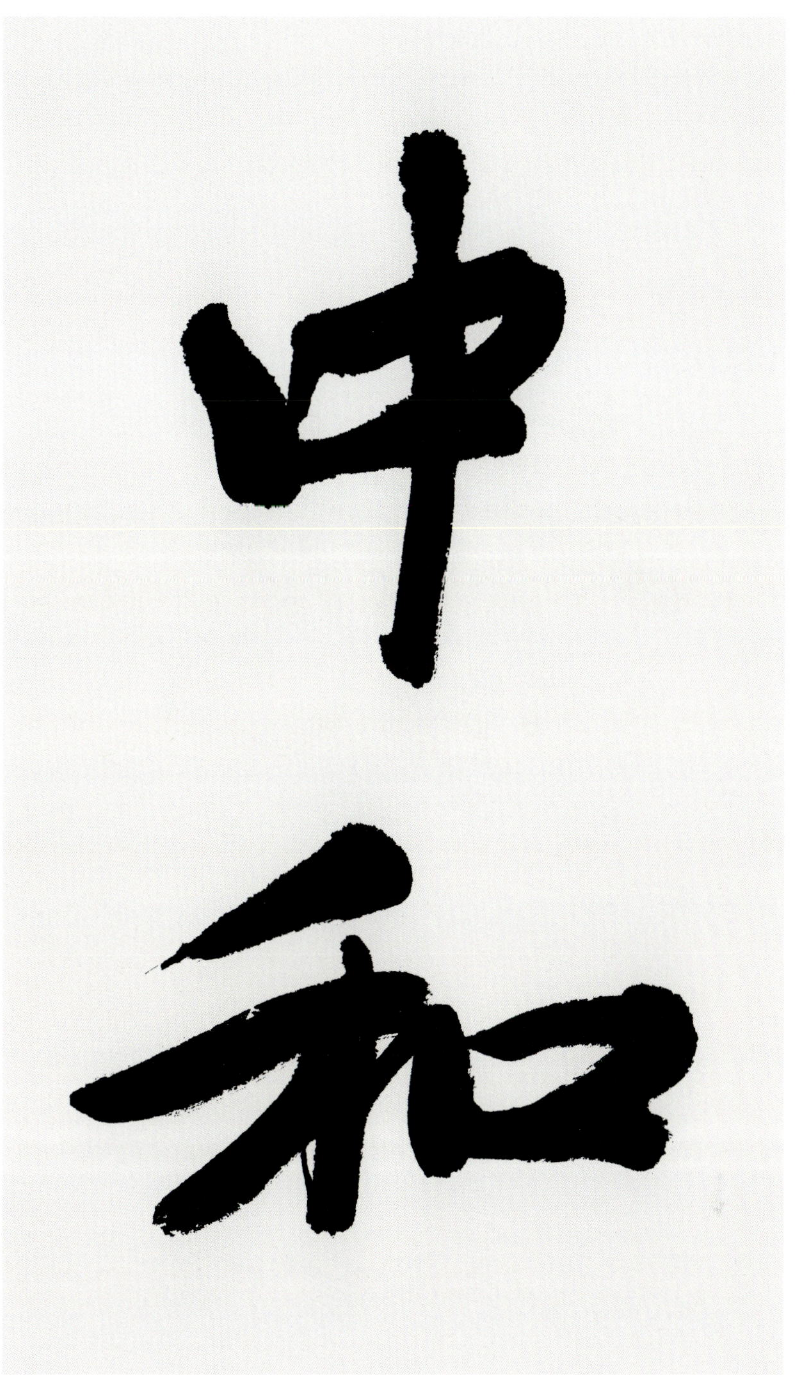

Fan Covering: A form of calligraphy written on fans or their paper coverings.

Example: 龍 (Traditional Chinese character of 龙, dragon)

The dragon is a legendary mythical creature, typically portrayed as a long, scaled, serpentine creatures with four legs and in control over water, rainfall, hurricane, and floods. In ancient China, the dragon was often a symbol of the emperor.

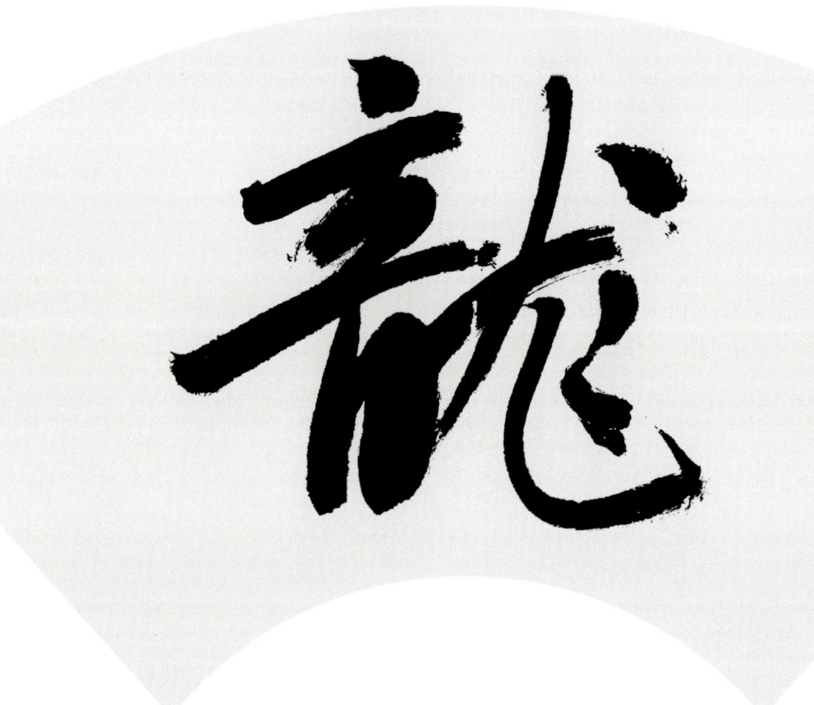

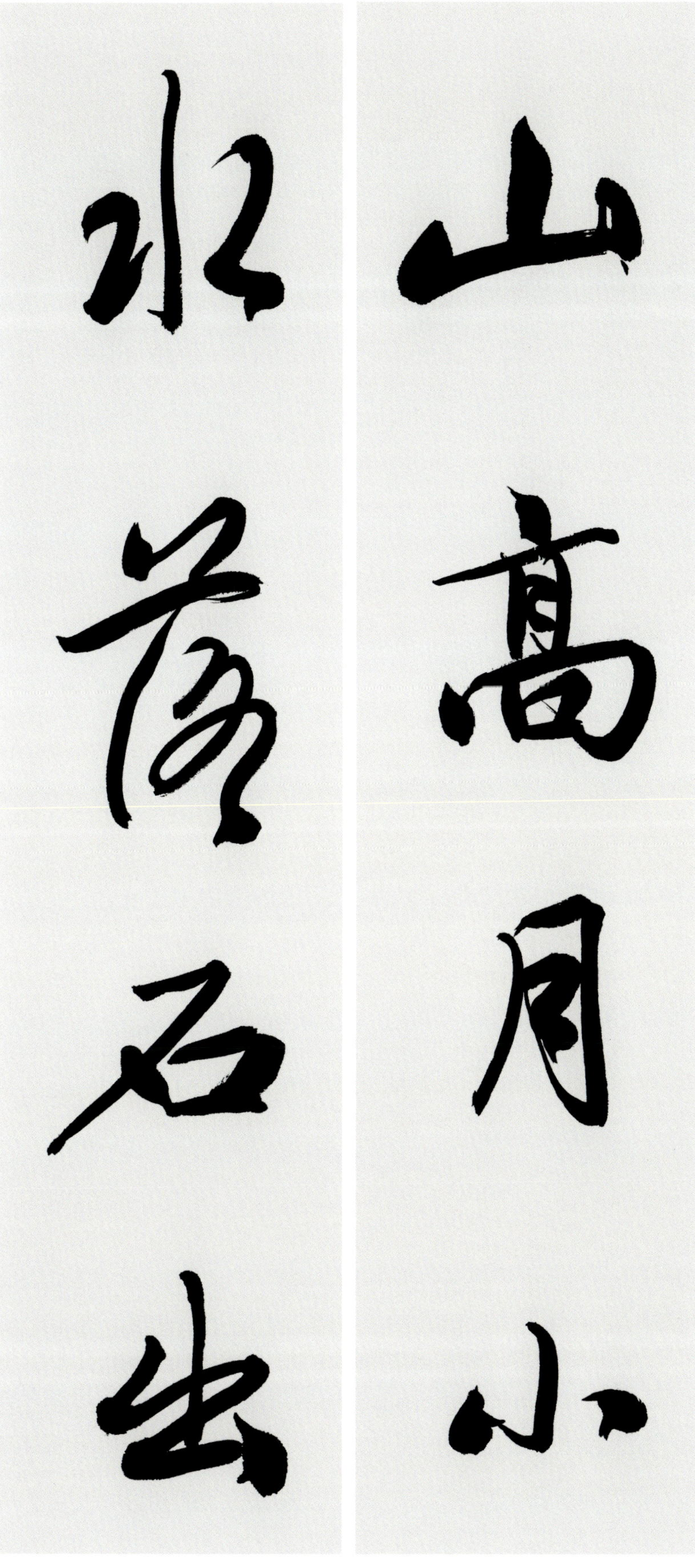

Couplet: An antithetical pair of lines normally hung on the sides of doors, in halls, or on pillars. It usually consists of two lines that rhyme and have the same meter. A special, widely seen type of couplet is the spring couplet, which is used as a New Year's decoration that expresses happy and hopeful thoughts for the coming year.

Example: 山高月小，水落石出

The couplet means that the Red Cliffs was so steep that the moon seemed so far away, so rugged that stones were revealed as the water ebbed.

Appendices

Bibliography

20 shiji shufa yanjiu congshu [20th Century Calligraphic Studies Series]. Shanghai: Shanghai shuhua chubanshe, 2000.

Jin Bo, *Sanxitang fatie teji zhiqi—Zhao Mengfu* [San Xi Tang Model Calligraphy (7th volume)]. Guangxi: Guangxi meishu shubanshe, 2006.

Jin Kaicheng and Wang Yuechuan, *Zhongguo shufa wenhua daguan* [A Grand Exposition of Chinese Calligraphic Culture]. Beijing: Beijing daxue chubanshe, 1995.

Jin Xuzhi, *Zhongguo shufa meixue* [Aesthetics in Chinese Calligraphy]. Nanjing: Jiangsu wenyi chubanshe, 1994.

Liang Piyun, *Zhongguo shufa dacidian* [Dictionary of Chinese Calligraphy Styles]. Hongkong: Xianggang shupu chubanshe; Guangzhou: Guangdong renmin chubanshe, 1987.

Lidai shufa lunwenxuan [Essays on Calligraphy in Different Dynasties]. Shanghai: Shanghai shuhua chubanshe, 1979.

Liu Heng, *Zhongguo shufashi* [History of Chinese Calligraphy]. Nanjing: Jiangsu jiaoyu chubanshe, 2002.

Sun Baowen, *Zhaomengfu shu qianhou chibifu* [First and Second Odes to Red Cliffs Written by Zhao Mengfu]. Shanghai: Shanghai cishu chubanshe, 2012.

Wen Shihua, *Zhaomengfu qianhou chibifu* [First and Second Odes to Red Cliffs Written by Zhao Mengfu]. Nanchang: Jiangxi meishu chubanshe, 2011.

Xue Haiyang, *Zhaomengfu qianhou chibifu* [First and Second Odes to Red Cliffs Written by Zhao Mengfu]. Zhengzhou: Henan meishu chubanshe, 2007

Yin Falu, *Guwen guanzhi yizhu* [Annotations to Ultimate Collection of Ancient Essays]. Changchun: Jinlin renmin chubanshe, 1981.

Yuan zhaomengfu qianhou chibifu [First and Second Odes to Red Cliffs Written by Zhao Mengfu of Yuan Dynasty], Shanghai: Shanghai shuhua chubanshe, 2004.

Zhang Guohong, *Zhaomengfu shufa yishu* [Art of Calligraphy of Zhao Mengfu]. Shanghai: Shanghai daxue chuabanshe, 2009.

Zhang Xigeng, *Xingshu shijiang* [Ten Lectures on Semi-Cursive Script]. Shanghai: Shanghai shuhua chubanshe, 2003.

Zhaomengfu shufa pinzhen [Appreciation of Zhao Mengfu's Calligraphic Works]. Shanghai: Shanghai shuhua chubanshe, 2007.

Index of Calligraphers and Works

Glossary

Chinese calligraphy ***zhongguo shufa*** **中国书法**
- clerical script *lishu* 隶书
- cursive script *caoshu* 草书
- drum-shaped stone block inscription *shiguwen* 石鼓文
- inscription on ancient bronze object *jinwen* 金文
- large seal script *dazhuan* 大篆
- oracle bone inscription *jiaguwen* 甲骨文
- regular script *kaishu* 楷书
- running-cursive script *xingcaoshu* 行草书
- running-regular script *xingkaishu* 行楷书
- semi-cursive script *xingshu* 行书
- small seal script *xiaozhuan* 小篆

Chinese calligraphy style ***shuti*** **书体**
- Slender Gold Style of Calligraphy *shoujinti* 瘦金体
- Yan-style calligraphy *yanti* 颜体
- Zhao-style calligraphy *zhaoti* 赵体

form of calligraphic composition ***zhangfa yangshi*** **章法样式**
- central scroll *zhongtang* 中堂
- couplet *duilian* 对联
- fan covering *shanmian* 扇面
- horizontally hung scroll *hengfu* 横幅

basic writing techniques ***jiben bifa*** **基本笔法**
- begin the stroke *qibi* 起笔
- end the stroke *shoubi* 收笔
- lift the brush *tibi* 提笔
- press the brush *dunbi* 顿笔
- wield the brush *xingbi* 行笔

eight principles of the Character Yong ***yongzi bafa*** **永字八法**
- dot *dian* 点
- hook *gou* 钩
- horizontal *heng* 横
- left-falling stroke *pie* 撇
- perpendicular *shu* 竖
- raise *ti* 提
- short slant *duanpie* 短撇
- wave *na* 捺

four treasures of the study ***wenfang sibao*** **文房四宝**
- ink *mo* 墨
  - carbon soot *xuanyan* 选烟
  - oil soot *youyan* 油烟
  - pine soot *songyou* 松油
- ink slab *yan* 砚
- paper *zhi* 纸
  - bamboo paper *yuanshuzhi* 元书纸
  - mulberry paper *pizhi* 皮纸
  - rice paper *xuanzhi* 宣纸
    - half-ripe rice paper *banshuxuan* 半熟宣
    - raw rice paper *shengxuan* 生宣
    - ripe rice paper *shuxuan* 熟宣
  - silk paper *juan* 绢
- writing brush *maobi* 毛笔
  - big brush *changfeng* 长锋
  - hard hairs *yinghao* 硬毫
  - medium brush *zhongfeng* 中锋
  - mixed hairs *jianhao* 兼毫
  - small brush *duanfeng* 短锋
  - soft hairs *ruanhao* 软毫

Dynasties in Chinese History

Xia Dynasty（夏）	2070 – 1600 BC
Shang Dynasty（商）	1600 – 1046 BC
Zhou Dynasty（周）	1046 – 256 BC
Western Zhou Dynasty（西周）	1046 – 771 BC
Eastern Zhou Dynasty（东周）	770 – 256 BC
Spring and Autumn Period（春秋）	770 – 476 BC
Warring States Period（战国）	475 – 221 BC
Qin Dynasty（秦）	221 – 206 BC
Han Dynasty（汉）	206 BC – 220 AD
Western Han Dynasty（西汉）	206 BC – 25 AD
Eastern Han Dynasty（东汉）	25 – 220
Three Kingdoms（三国）	220 – 280
Wei（魏）	220 – 265
Shu Han（蜀）	221 – 263
Wu（吴）	222 – 280
Jin Dynasty（晋）	265 – 420
Western Jin Dynasty（西晋）	265 – 316
Eastern Jin Dynasty（东晋）	317 – 420
Northern and Southern Dynasties（南北朝）	420 – 589
Southern Dynasties（南朝）	420 – 589
Northern Dynasties（北朝）	439 – 581
Sui Dynasty（隋）	581 – 618
Tang Dynasty（唐）	618 – 907
Five Dynasties and Ten Kingdoms（五代十国）	907 – 960
Five Dynasties（五代）	907 – 960
Ten Kingdoms（十国）	902 – 979
Song Dynasty（宋）	960 – 1279
Northern Song Dynasty（北宋）	960 – 1127
Southern Song Dynasty（南宋）	1127 – 1279
Liao Dynasty（辽）	916 – 1125
Jin Dynasty（金）	1115 – 1234
Xixia Dynasty（西夏）	1038 – 1227
Yuan Dynasty（元）	1279 – 1368
Ming Dynasty（明）	1368 – 1644
Qing Dynasty（清）	1644 – 1911